S0-BYY-226

BRIFFAULT'S
PASSCHENDAELE

BRIFFAULT'S PASSCHENDAELE

Arts, Empathy, and the First World War

Phil McCray

Rudi Publishing

Copyright © 2014 by Phil McCray
All rights reserved

Published in the United States by Rudi Publishing

Hardcover ISBN 978-0-945213-32-1
Paperback ISBN 978-0-945213-34-5
E Book ISBN 978-0-945213-36-9

Library of Congress Control Number: 2014949226

Special thanks to the William Ready Division of Archives
and Research Collections, McMaster University Library
in Hamilton, Ontario; and the British Library in London.

Photo Credits:
Cover photo by Frank Hurley (soldiers of an Australian 4th Division
field artillery brigade on a duckboard track passing through
Chateau Wood near Hooge in the Ypres salient, 29 October 1917);
Robert Briffault (page 185) courtesy of McMaster University;
Charles Waterman Lawry (page 187) courtesy of Cynthia Lawry;
Wyndham Lewis photo by George Charles Beresford (page 190), 1913.

Book and cover design by Terri A. Boekhoff

CONTENTS

PREFACE

In the Great War, the 1916 Battle of Verdun resulted in a
quarter-million deaths. On the first day of the Battle of the Somme,
also in 1916, 19,000 British soldiers were killed, and the battle claimed
300,000 British, German, and French lives. After these battles,
there was nothing to be gained by fighting on, but English 'pluck' rotted
itself into English intransigence, the German people, driven to starvation,
had not yet refused to support the army and the war,
and the killing mowed on for two more years.
Schlachten. Slaughter.

The First World War was engaged in the name of strategic alliances.
Most of the war was fought in Flanders and in eastern France, across
facing, immobile trenches. The strategy of attrition demands that though
it take a million killed to kill a million one, that shall be called victory.
Across Europe, sixteen million people died.

There were three major battles at Ypres, a medieval Belgian city
near the coast. The third of these, in the summer and fall of 1917,
is often simply called "Passchendaele."
Passchendaele was a horror of trench warfare and the grimmest fruit
of the strategy of pure attrition: 600,000 men died.
There are today 618 British burial grounds and ossuaries in Europe
including 137 British cemeteries in the immediate Ypres vicinity.
Beyond these interments at Passchendaele,
90,000 bodies were never found.

The significance of the First World War is now comprehensible chiefly by way of the printed word and the reproduced image. The sound of the voice of the soldiers is gone from the lips and the tongue, and will never bear that peculiar dimension of language as it is spoken directly to us by someone who was there. For us the war must exist forever in an abstract and slighter remove. Archivists, museum curators, and memoirists have seemed to reduce the war to an act of commemoration, and left it at that. Historians too seemed to have considered the war only as a *story*, a discrete set of facts and observations about a particular skein of causes and effects. Social memory itself seemed indifferent to the barbarity that produced the body counts.

If we are to ever get beyond the basic story of the war, the surest way to access the madness and horror is by a personal route of faithful, even if idiosyncratic, empathy: if I had been there, what would my feelings have been? What would I have done? My own access to the war a hundred years after its time, and the way in which its horrors came down to me, was through the literary, humanist, artistic, and socialist perspectives, and these frames of reference are the same by which I learned the craft of empathy. For better or worse, the only manner of conveyance I really trust is sympathetic, artistic expression.

I was also fascinated by the very process by which, to my surprise, I had worked myself into an anxious state of mind concerning a subject for which I had previously no interest and about which I had only the most cursory knowledge. But I would come to believe that the war is part of our collective unconscious, and its lesson of what men can be made to do to other men has seeped into our spirit whether or not we ever think of the political events of 1914-1918.

A number of books and artworks describe the war each in their own way, yet all say the same thing: though in the field there were countless acts of bravery and personal audacity, the war itself was unnecessary and absurd.

The Second World War—my father's generation's war—always seemed comprehensible: a terrible scourge had to be arrested, and fearsome measures proceeded to accomplish that. It was a tale that tracked

neatly from beginning to end. The First World War lacked such compre-
hensibility, and its course and matters were illogical; every aspect of it
seemed deranged and pitiless. Yet, paradoxically, accounts and memoirs
of the war produced some exquisite writing, as if the fearsome events
had pressed language itself to its most beautiful possible form.

Some years ago, I immersed myself in the literature of the British
literary Moderns, particularly the Vorticists, with their preoccupation
with angularity, the mechanical perspective, and futurism. The writers
associated with Modernism generally, and with Vorticism especially,
participated in or were deeply affected by the war. Some understood
their creative work as an effort to resolve the darker implications of the
disaster in a relevant, literate form. At about the same time I was reading
the Vorticists, I was discovering in the writings of the cultural anthro-
pologist and novelist Robert Briffault exemplifications of the power of
literature and socialism to cultivate one's empathy. Briffault served as a
medical officer in Flanders, and was forced to rationalize and integrate
his literary and practical worlds. We find relevances, connections, and
contexts wherever we may, and these structures and patterns of empathy—the grammar of our sensibilities—are the only realities that will ever
really matter to us.

i.

TRUCULENT SCHOLARSHIP

. . . the songs came up from Spain
the songs came up from Africa . . .

Robert Briffault (de Chancel) was born in 1873 in Nice, France, the son of a minister of Louis Napoleon III. He was, consequently, raised in a privileged and cosmopolitan atmosphere of culture, political power, and learning. After his father's death, his Scottish mother and he settled in New Zealand, where he was educated and was awarded a medical degree at the University of Christchurch. Briffault served as a surgeon in the First World War at Gallipoli and in Flanders, at age forty-four. He was twice gassed and twice wounded, and was decorated for conspicuous bravery. After the war, he ceased practicing medicine, studied widely, and wrote novels and treatises arrayed across the subjects of the decay of European culture; nationalism and war; Provençal troubadour poetry; cultural anthropology and art; the matriarchal origins of societies; and the Moorish wellsprings of western European culture. His principal work, the three-volume *The Mothers*, bore comparison with James Frazer's *The Golden Bough*, though it never achieved that work's readership or esteem.

By unanimous judgment, Briffault was a fabulously learned and inventive thinker, yet also an overbearing and difficult personality. He was a communist and an atheist, yet he was a dandy who dressed well and accustomed himself to the fine and cultured living he had known as a child. He had many mistresses, and his behavior toward his second wife (the American translator Herma Hoyt Briffault[1]) struck all his acquaintances as, at best, insufficiently kind. He once refused to promenade in Cap d'Antibes after having broken his walking cane, appearing without which might have signaled that he was something less than aristocratic. Briffault dedicated one of his books "to no one," since he had written it entirely without the patronage he knew he had deserved. His intellectual arrogance can be inferred by knowing that when Briffault was a boy, a guest in the family home placed his hands on the young lad's head, and to illustrate a point he was making about the brave future, said: "He might be the one." The guest was Friederich Nietzsche, and it is unlikely that such a bestowal would be soon forgotten by an incipient egocentric.

Briffault and Herma lived in occupied Paris during the Second World War, near the Luxembourg Gardens. He was arrested twice and lived in considerable hardship, yet he wrote and studied constantly. At one point Herma buried one of his manuscripts in the garden so that it would not be confiscated by the Nazis. Due to his status as a British subject and communist, he was unable to enter the United States on Herma's passport. After the war, he wandered Europe's ravaged cities alone, chiefly to be near the great libraries that were so necessary for his cultural research. He died in Hastings, England in 1948, and his will left his material possessions not to his wife, but to his Russian mistress Mme Marina Stalio. The rights to his literary estate were granted to his surviving daughter, Joan Briffault de Hackelberg, who had emigrated to Chile. Though he chose to become a British citizen, and served in His Majesty's armed forces during the Great War, Briffault had a life-long loathing for England and its rampant imperialism, racism, and subjugation of citizens by class. Some of his invective took the form of bitter ejaculations, and appeared to some of his acquaintances to be more a sort of a psychological reflex than rational opinion. From the trenches near Ypres in 1917 he wrote of the "obscene hypocrisy" of London and its complacent citizenry, the vulgarity of the war profiteers, and the distortions of the mendacious press. When the Munich Pact was signed in 1938, he returned his World War One decorations to the King. Yet he wanted to be buried in England, that is to say, not in France, and not in Florence, the cities in which he passed many fecund years of his life. He evinced disdain for property, yet received without demur the material gifts of persons who offered him support. Similarly, he claimed that marriage and monogamy were utterly ridiculous, yet he was married twice; he professed the strongest of faiths in the common man, whose public behavior he could not stand. That Briffault was able to simultaneously entertain two completely opposite compulsions in his mind may suggest that he was capable of enormous feats of genius—as genius was defined by Aristotle—or provides support of the conclusion that these ambivalences were related to the narcoleptic seizures he experienced all his life.

Briffault was not known to have done any actual field research in cultural anthropology, hence his emphasis on the matriarchal structure of culture was purely theoretical. Ashley Montagu and other intellectuals were, however, uniformly amazed by his reading and his astounding ability to recollect and cite resources. Montagu wrote: "As a man of imagination—undisciplined imagination—Briffault was brilliant. As a man he was a failure. Temperament, as Voltaire remarked, is Fate." Many of his peers also questioned his conclusions, and regarded the process and assumptions of his scholarship as quite outlandish. Even Gordon Rattray Taylor, in his introduction to a later, condensed version of *The Mothers*, struggled to find indisputable value in Briffault's theories, noting that the author had tried to generalize when generalization was impossible, and that some of his intellectual methodology was altogether flawed.

The Great War showed Briffault at his most disciplined and stable, and he was by all accounts an amiable-enough colleague. His New Zealand medical degree was in chirurgy, a form of medical care specializing in manual and instrumental treatments. In the aid tents this was especially appropriate, where countless summary amputations were necessary. The equipment used in amputations might appear to a wounded soldier as brute hacksaws, spears, and topiary loppers, but a physician's resolve was the one source of order. At times physicians were so overwhelmed that mortal decisions were made instantaneously, and wounded soldiers whose lives might have been saved had to be left outside the crowded surgery tents to expire. The medical conditions were horrifying, worsened by the proximity of the bomb blasts and bullets. Over one thousand British doctors, and fifteen hundred German medical officers were killed during the war.

Returning to private life after the Great War, Briffault's inflexibility relating to social decorum, his rigorous intellectual standards, and his characteristic obduracy resulted in numerous personal and professional quarrels. He once behaved scandalously at a religious mass at Chartres, and was so queasy about public physicality that he forced Herma to wear a robe when swimming. He traveled from California to New York via Niagara Falls, but appears to have been wholly indifferent to that grand spectacle of nature. He was mad for Wagner's operas and would play the radio at full volume; he "abominated Mozart and Bach." He exaggerated small nuisances and delighted in contravening authority in even the smallest matters. He admitted to being emotionally undone by the death of his favorite daughter Muriel, and he was so estranged from his son Lister that Herma does not appear to have known of the latter's existence until after she and Briffault were married.[2]

Robert Briffault was frequently poor (and at the end of his life entirely destitute) but he continued to try to live the life of a dandy and a connoisseur. Both he and Herma often declared that they "were not worthy of being communists," suggesting the purely parlor nature of their political beliefs. The 1930s and the years of the Second World War presented their own difficulties for his scholarly career, and he seems to have regarded all editors, publishers, and translators as his natural adversaries. His relationships with his several mistresses was a strange tangle of invidious chaos. He had an imperial sense of his role in the intellectual life of the world, felt aggrieved by his lack of fame, and very strongly believed that he was owed patronage by whomever might be capable of providing him with money, housing, or access to publication.

And, like his alter ego Julian Bern in the *Europa* novels, he had a flair for associating with persons of notoriety. In Paris and on the Côte d'Azur during and after the Second World War his social relations were varied, though none appear to have significantly satisfied or challenged him. He became especially close with William and Jenny Bradley, the Paris publishers of Gertrude Stein and Henry Miller, and with Stuart Gilbert, the friend and scholar of James Joyce. Briffault was a careful reader of Proust and Joyce. He was acquainted with Sylvia Beach, the doyenne of the Paris English-language bookshop, Shakespeare and Company. The literary entrepreneur Maurice Girodias was eventually able to publish some of Briffault's literary fiction, but only by emphasizing its decadence and sexual liberty. The Vieillards were companionable neighbors of the Briffaults during the Second World War, but found their elaborate relationships with cats to be an immense facade.

In England, Herma and Briffault relied on Stella Bowen, the never-quite-wife of Ford Madox Ford; Bowen loaned Briffault a country cottage, in which he corrected the galleys of his last literary work, *The New Life of Mr. Martin*. The art collector Eric Estorick described Briffault as a "son of a bitch," yet he was strongly attracted to the older author. Lawrence F. Koons, who would write the preface to a 1965 edition of Briffault's *The Troubadours* wrote: "Like everyone else, Estorick paid tribute to Briffault's intellect, his erudition, his ability to absorb unbelievable amounts of information, synthesize it, and express the conclusions in remarkable English."

One of the most curious relations in Briffault's life may be also the most telling. After the Second World War—Briffault is in his seventies and unwell—he establishes an *affair de cœur* with Malrika Phillips, the young wife of Rodney Phillips, a wealthy actor and publisher. Phillips had once provided funds for Briffault, who sometimes lived with the Phillips family. Rodney's occasional gifts allowed the old writer to travel, and to alternate his periods of poverty with stays in the four-star hotels to which he had once been accustomed. Phillips formed a sort of social/literary clique around himself, peopled with modish "homosexuals, ingénues, and starlets." Koons writes: "Malrika had spent the war years in North Africa, and returned to France in 1945, where she took up with a bunch of *rive gauche* characters, wore long hair and blue jeans, practiced free love and all the concomitant affectations. Briffault sought to save her from the phony existentialist milieu in which she was swimming." Malrika was the daughter of Marie (Marevna) Bronislava Vorobieff-Stebelska, often referred to as the first female cubist painter, who had an ill-fated dalliance with the Mexican painter Diego Rivera. Briffault's relationship with Malrika was tortured and intensely erotic. He once signed a letter to her with "I kiss you in a place where I won't get any lipstick on myself," and "I am dying of the desire to make love to you, and at the same time I want to scream at you, to insult you." Trained as an exotic dancer and schooled partly by Isadora Duncan, "Malrika Rivera" became an actress, and appeared with Julie Christie in the 1965 film *Darling*. Briffault also befriended Marevna on the Riviera, and made futile attempts to gain the favor of and pecuniary support of Malrika's mother. In the last two years of his life, and tubercular, Briffault's exalted appreciation of carnality and *amor* devolved into an obsession with pornography, though his writings suggest that this was but a mystical expression of the forces of femininity which had all his life informed both his spirit and his intellectual foundations. Herma Briffault did eventually file for a divorce (never legalized) but she was insistent that Briffault was a great man, and that he had been ill-treated by members of the intellectual firmament. She strove to assure potential biographers that he was, despite countless acts of nonfeasance, brilliant, true, and good. Malrika, too, knew that Briffault's behavior might obscure his work and stain his reputation, and pleaded that Koons would "be kind to Robert."

Though the last several years of his life were colored with disorder and conflict, he was, during his service in the First World War, exceptionally dedicated to his medical responsibilities. Despite days without sleep or proper nourishment, he tended faithfully to the maimed and dying, in a way that might even have suggested a kind of maternal care, a Whitman-esque sympathetic love. He particularly distinguished himself by leaving the relative safety of the aid tents, and venturing into the shell holes of No Man's Land to provide care to the wounded. Dandies are not normally associated with such brazen acts of courage and selflessness, suggesting yet another view of Briffault's personality. This dichotomy parallels in some ways the average soldier, who exceeded himself with superhuman and often heroic feats during the war, but then returned home to a domestic, bourgeois life. The war extracted previously unknown elements from a person's interior character.

In Briffault's view, after the Great War the British and Russian soldiers returned to the motherland and its cant and hypocrisy, to a redeemed and rampant Capitalism, or a chancred socialism. The German soldier returned to the fatherland and its eternal sense of grievance and belligerence, and eventually to its rapturous orgy of nationalism. The war had been a perpetuation, rather than a collapse, of the determination of a person's value by class. Few subversive habits were immediately brought back from the battlefields to the major cities of Europe. Chronic servitude and privilege were intact; breeding's superiority over merit was not shaken. The war did set free numerous genres of aesthetic Modernism, but these did not often penetrate to the lives of the shopkeepers or servants who had obeyed the call of the Empire. The war had actually stultified individuality for members of the middle and working class, by reaffirming their tractability.

A pass through the titles of Briffault's books accurately reveals the scope of his interests and his political and moral inflections. His first book, published in 1919 (and largely composed, amazingly, during his service in the war), was nothing less than *The Making of Humanity (Rational Evolution)*, followed by *Psyche's Lamp: A Re-evaluation of Psychological Principles as a Foundation of All Thought*. He then published *The Decline and Fall of the British Empire*, (which *Time* magazine reviewed, declaring that "its criticism is so undiscriminating that readers may fear Briffault would not like the English even if they were good"), *Breakdown: The Collapse of Traditional Civilization*, and the three-volume *The Mothers: A Study of the Origins of Sentiments and Institutions (The Matriarchal Theory of Social*

Origins). Briffault argued in all these books that it is only when we are able to "shake off the dead hand of traditional heredity that we reach our highest potential." He wrote a play about Don Juan, in which one might infer clues to Briffault's sexual temperament and amatory habits, and he published articles that appeared in the leftist English and French periodical literature, including such essays as "The Nature of Life," "Impersonality," and "Science and Metaphysics." Critics and readers have debated Briffault's choice of *The Mothers* as the title for his magnum opus, citing its obvious Freudian implications, especially in relation to the author's fixation on sexuality. Mme Stalio contended, however, that the titular influence had to do with Goethe's preoccupation with a more ethereal maternality, as in his poems *Die Mutters*. In the mid 1930s, Briffault turned to fiction, with *Europa, The Days of Ignorance*, and *Europa in Limbo*, the first becoming an unexpected bestseller. Both books described the decay and collapse of European culture prior to World War One.

Briffault's own mother, a plain and sturdy Scotswoman, figures neither overtly nor indirectly in his own novels, correspondence, biographical notes, or philosophical writings, except that his major, symphonic work of cultural anthropology was so titled. That matriarchal origins of culture were not the only force of the female that obsessed him was attested to by what his friends call his "numerous" mistresses. The bon vivant who appreciated fine champagnes and perfumes did not always extend such generosity to his paramours or to his two wives, and his misogynistic habits suggest further ambivalences of mind regarding mothers and women.

He returned to cultural anthropology with *Reasons for Anger, Marriage Past and Present*, and *Sin and Sex*. ("Puritan tradition, combined with Christian management of adolescence, has converted the sexual life of civilized men and women into a neurosis.") A novel followed, *Fandango*, (published in an American edition with a lurid pulp cover as *Carlotta*) which concerned the Spanish Civil War, Moorish history, and communism. Briffault always counseled, when trying to determine the direction of the world: "Watch Spain."[3]

During the Second World War in Paris (perhaps with funds from the German occupying force, though he was a virulent anti-Nazi) he published three pamphlets: *L'Angleterre et l'Egypt*, *La Fable anglaise*, and *La Troisième Guerre Mondiale*. When the German edition of *Europa* was burned by the Nazis, he said "it is the highest honour I have yet had paid to me." In his last incredible years of poverty, wandering, and research, he composed the philological study *Les Troubadours et le sentiment Romanesque*, and the novel *The New Life of Mr. Martin*, the latter a form of visionary fantasy. During the Great War Briffault had observed hundreds of men at the blink of passage from life to death. In his last piece of sustained writing, he recapitulates this fleeting alloy of being and nothingness in a fragile essence that occupies neither time nor space.

Briffault's novels tend to be Voltairean in nature, as they broadly stage-manage his personal polemics. Story lines are charted along necessary philosophical and political vectors, rather than sculpted by the natural vicissitudes of characters' lives. It is, however, masterful how efficiently in the *Europa* novels brief appearances are made by Henry James, Rasputin, Mata Hari, James Joyce, and Vladimir Lenin. As representatives of the matriarchal center, both Zena, the fey Russian princess (who perishes), and Eleanor (who will give birth at the very end of the novel), are intensely self-reliant. They are among the strongest women in modern literature, putting Daisy Buchanan and Nicole Diver rather in the shade.

Zena is a derivative soul of a Russian girl Briffault knew, by whom his heart was affected in a painful and disorienting way. He kept a mistress during his medical service in the war in Flanders, named Julia; she was the prototype of Keetje, and had a monumental psychological effect on the author. Keetje is perhaps Briffault's most significant female archetype. Her life is vibrantly portrayed in *Europa in Limbo*. Keetje appears first as a scruffy waif-gamine displaced by the war, who later navigates through the broken world to the highest levels of intrigue and power. Keetje's natural understanding of her sexuality-as-power expresses one of Briffault's chief beliefs, the authority inherent in the self-defined female: the hoyden as rulebreaker, the transgressive, cynical spy. As a matter of critical importance, there are moments when Keetje is sullen and bored; she is comprehensively uninterested in anything the world may be up to. To her the war is merely bothersome. She is aloof, cool. Her disinvolvement is the only strategy that ever wholly succeeds in Briffault's novels. She implicitly understands that she will have to create for herself the only set of forms and responses that can ever have any real meaning.

The Troubadours, published in 1945, is a philological excursion into the poetic song of twelfth-century Provence's medieval discipline of courtly love. The book's central premise, crucial to understanding Briffault's principles of western intellectual life, is derived from two key chapters in The Mothers. "It was under the influence of Arabian and Moorish revival of culture," according to Briffault, "and not in the fifteenth century, that the real renaissance took place. Spain and not Italy was the cradle of the rebirth of Europe." Provençal troubadour lyric "answered the mood of a feudal society newly awakened to a sense of its native uncouthness by contact with the luxury of the Orient." Chaucer and Dante inherited the forms of the troubadour song, the latter declaring that the "poet's first duty [was] to keep jealous ward over the purity of his native tongue." The lady was always central in Provençal writing, always, though she was not exclusively a holy queen or sexual siren. The troubadour was a vagabond, whose well-being depended on his or her ability to create salubrious lyrics that would give pleasing form to the era's new conception of love. This illustrates the process by which a moral, sensual love is degenerated by the church's prescriptive and starved forms into the Albigensian Crusade against an aesthetic, autochthonous sentiment of sympathetic liberalism. The pigment of the poetry's field is the refined love of the lady, crafted into new shades and spectrums of surpassing sophistication. In keeping with his irascible and highly opinionated understanding of historical facts and cultural expression, Briffault was often irritated out of measure with those persons who perpetuated the idea that the Renaissance was not wholly indebted to Moorish and Islamic principles.

Briffault's last book was *The New Life of Mr. Martin* (1947), which cites as epigraph Arthur Symons' remark that "We have no longer the mental attitude of those to whom a story was but a story." It is a book, published thirty years after Passchendaele, Briffault said "he had to write," though he understood that it would be a commercial failure. It was dedicated to Kyle Crichton (better known as the Marxist columnist Robert Forsythe), with whom Briffault, according to form, later quarreled. Elements of most of his polemics in several of his books are here plainly stated. The tale presents a fabulist's cinematic adventures, the sort of writing that corresponded to his intense and refined enjoyment of what he called a "voluptuous" meal. The saga consists of florid imposture, impossible grandeur, and magnificent anti-fascism.

One might presume that as Briffault tended the maimed soldiers in a trance of exhaustion and despair, he could have regarded 1917's Flanders hell as the very worst that man could ever imagine, yet it raised the possibility that an equal glory might have been realized had England been properly acculturated and the Moorish philosophies had been fulfilled. Sheila, the female protagonist in *The New Life of Mr. Martin*, ventures *alone* across the North African desert; it is she to whom alone is revealed the ineffably magnificent brilliance of the Moorish libraries, and to whom is entrusted the utterance of the Arabic word *horm*, referring to the "privacies of life and mind," that form a central tenet of Briffault's crypto-Emersonianism. The contradiction of his life and his work renders Briffault a strange sort of proto Marxist-feminist, though his eccentric, freestyle sort of genius prevented any school of thought from claiming him as one of their own. Excepting Briffault's flash of renown with the publication of *Europa*, and a current faddish reference to his observations regarding matriarchy, he is absent from both literary and anthropological history. The centennial of the Great War may occasion exposure to his medical service during the war, but few now know his name.

Mr. Martin's sublime ethereality, combined with the author's tortuous and combative relation with the ways of the world, may form the most apt understanding of Robert Briffault. As he professed in all aspects of his personal life and intellectual work, the central and elemental truth resides in the half-real Beatrice, Laura, and Melisande. There is always a chimerical woman in Briffault's work, and usually a tomboy. This last novel's first and final images are depictions of a woman's fulsome breasts.

ii.

THE SCRIPTS OF HELL

The Third Battle of Ypres, commonly called "Passchendaele," was fought from the 31st of July to the 11th of November, 1917. Flanders rains converted the flatlands into a sea of mud, preventing all standard forms of military engagement, yet diminishing not at all the colossal death count. Many thousands of men choked to death on gas, succumbed to sepsis, drowned in quickmud shell holes, or went mad. Individually, German and British soldiers performed heroically despite the appalling conditions and the obscene slaughter. Canadian troops eventually took possession of the ruined village of Passchendaele, a sort of victory was implied, and the "theatre of war" moved on to other ambiguous locales and continued its slow decay towards armistice. Passchendaele, the Battle, slipped into history, but few at the time dared call it evitable or useless. The battle gained a minuscule amount of land for the Allied Forces, which later was simply relinquished to the German Army.

The 1914–1918 war was an apotheosis of nationalist intent. It was directed by plutocratic primogeniturists and their gentlemen toadies, relying on cartographic and coronetic simplicities. Its rationale was founded in the minds of perhaps one hundred men. It was a war that depended on primitive patterns in ancient societies that had derived from the fiefdom's dehumanization of work-units, factitious religions, and a people who had not yet learned resistance or even dissent. It was, therefore, a fashion of medieval war, and it signified, as Ezra Pound said of James Joyce's *Ulysses*, an end, not a beginning. As if to accentuate the fact that the Great War was a *grand guignol* of death, immediately after the cessation of hostilities, in a cruel Malthusian parody, twenty million persons died in the Spanish influenza epidemic.

Belgian Flanders was the perfect venue for such a war. For many centuries various greeds and vanities had played out their *auto-da-fés* on its unforgiving flatlands. Its cities, by contrast, had been citadels of discretion and learning, and those venues of refined culture had served as the center of the western world. Amid lands that had hosted internecine battles of conquest and murder, fabrics and cloths of exquisite subtlety and beauty had been created, indicative that here the medieval mind was capable of blooming into one of surpassing grace.

Just prior to the war, the dominance of the wealthy classes appeared to be declining, and new art forms such as the Ballets Russes and *The Rite of Spring* seemed to promise an aesthetic breakthrough. Suffragette liberties and the emancipation of the common man's right to possess some of the wealth of society were first shadings toward modernity. The Great War smothered and postponed these innovations and inchoate rights. The writer and soldier Wyndham Lewis wrote that "the War has stopped Art dead." Yet after the war, literature and the fine arts seemed to proclaim that if the central moral code of humanity could be violated, as by the war, then almost anything one wanted to say or do should be possible. Modernist art was, at least partly, liberating painting, sculpture, and theatre from the prescriptive dictates of critics and academicians and turning the privilege of perception over to the viewer. Just as the flooding rains and war transformed the once-gracious farmlands of Flanders into a huge treeless bog and erased their bucolic beauty, so new art forms seemed to respond to the offense of the war by rejecting sylvan simplicities, and by forming original artworks created wholly from the mind of one artist's sensibility.

The majority of the men ferried across the English Channel, entrained, billeted, queued through mess tents, sickened, and killed, were culled from the trodden tides of England's immense service culture. Some of these folk had been so fixed in their subjection and so schooled to be invisible that, as servants in the trenches, they were pleased enough to have provided their master with a few moments of comfort and relief, in the form of hot tea, washed socks, or an extra glass of claret.

Soldiers did not expect to be remembered. They had been drawn into something monstrously large and beyond their understanding. None but the very few wished ever to be valorized. The most we can imagine them hoping for is that yet another light might be shined on the futility of mankind's massive departure from reason by means of bellicosity (even though the First World War guaranteed the Second, and the Second World War prophesies a Third).

The political war was never the soldiers' war. Mutual belligerence was betrothed because German *kultur* demanded it, and entrenched English class-docility and war-profiteering perpetuated it. English armament growth was the first response to German industrialization and modernized engineering, but the plainer folk of the combatant nations might never have imagined a reason to engage in arms. Episodes of battlefield fraternization among the soldiers revealed these particular irrelevancies, and even exposed the inconvenient truth that the British soldiers had more in common with the German than with the French. Societal prejudices and animosities directed at gastronomic vulgarians (the English) or unbathed syphilitics (the French) proved sturdier than the statements imposed by a toady press, or by the members of a costive general staff composed of stooges and flunkies. The soldiers did not initially hate their opponent soldiers, and the generals most often had gentlemanly respect for the tactics of their opponent generals. When the German air ace Manfred von Richthofen was shot down and killed near Vaux-sur-Somme in April of 1918, British officers served quite proudly as his pallbearers at the burial. (Foot soldiers might have resented such an honor.) The French artist and soldier Henri Gaudier-Brzeska nonchalantly met German soldiers in No Man's Land to exchange newspapers. Still, ineradicably, nationalism's bigoted chestnuts persisted: German soldiers' accounts uniformly portrayed the raiding English soldiers as "drunks." The French were cowards. German ridicule of the British trenches' inferior engineering was legitimate, and mattered a great deal to their pride. Fraternization proved the idiocy of nominal nationalism, revealed by the fact that some German soldiers who performed heroically in the First World War were in the Second exterminated: Jews.

In the trenches, men were instinctual. They were severed from their pasts, from catechism, from dogma. They were pure and often noble beasts of the violated natural world distilled into nerve nets, and no matters of cerebral abstraction were particularly useful. Writing letters home they tried to allay the concerns of their families by minimizing the misery and danger, but that will have been perhaps the extent of their identification with their former lives, when their most evident concerns had been with wage-earning, perhaps courtship, and the simple maintenance of forward progress. These letters reveal a telling juxtaposition, in which the soldiers revert to the idiom of their former lives, where they were usually subservient proletarians drowning in the very platitudes that substantiated the moral deception which got them into the trenches. They otherwise behaved with inherent, but suppressed, boldness and fellowship. A few commentators allege that there was a godly spirit in the trenches—not mustard gas or the reek of ratshit—but a benign divinity of immaculate protection and faith. But the sense in such platitudes eluded those trying to extract from the wide oceans of mud and malice the tiny impression (was it a conceit?) that represented to them the fond, far ideal of the rest of their lives. They survived or died according to chance, at the intersection of their motor instincts and the indifferent gravitational arch of a bullet or fragment of a shell.

The solder/writer Frederick Manning wrote:

> These apparently rude and brutal natures comforted, encouraged, and reconciled each other to fate, with a tenderness and tact which was more moving than anything in life. They had nothing; not even their own bodies, which had become mere implements of warfare. They turned from the wreckage and misery of life to an empty heaven, and from an empty heaven to the silence of their own hearts.

> They had been brought to the last extremity of hope, and they put
> their hands on each other's shoulders and said with a passionate con-
> viction that it would be all right, though they had faith in nothing
> but in themselves and in each other.

A similar realization occurred to Stuart Cloete, the South African novelist who served with the King's Own Yorkshire Light Infantry and the Cold-
stream Guards. Cloete was wounded at the Somme, and, horrified
by the conditions in the medical tents, lost control of his mind. Briefly
confined to a mental hospital, he returned to the front in 1917, was
again seriously wounded, and during his recovery stated that he needed
to go back into the war: "perhaps the war had made such an impression on me, it seemed the only reality, and only soldiers appeared to me
as people."

Most books about the war assign to memory the role of keeping the Great
War alive, at least, in the minds of those who are committed to understanding the scope of the human condition. This approach implies that memory
is somehow fixed, and something about which we may not have the right
to speculate. But Proust's Marcel reminds us that memory is a process, not
a lockbox, and we can begin to shift the war and its damages from its residence locked in the past, by remembering the challenge to a living person
of putting the war to the simple test of contemporaneity: what would I do in
an icy trench, ravaged with lice, rat bites, and depression, and made to climb
out of the hole and face a bullet that is meant for me in a way that is ines-
timably personal? Virtually every compilation of memoirs of the war by its
participants includes some form of "you had to be there to understand it."
Narrative—and by extension photographs and films—are therefore reduced
to a sort of hearsay, and none of us alive today can claim to know or feel
anything more about the war than we can understand as even a sympathetic
surveillant. One soldier noted that sorting through the many deaths he had
observed revealed that one pal's loss was met with a shrug and another's
was deeply grieved, and there was no accounting for the difference. Some
reverse affinity or charisma was at work, by which indifference became a

mechanism of mental survival. A survivor of the war might have a deeper relationship with a late soldier's ghost than with an acquaintance back home, and such an effect or condition cannot be paraphrased. These differences suggest fields of being that are outside memory. The empathy created within one's own mind (as with longing and fear) is always stronger than that acquired through our second-hand acquisition of narrative reports.

In twelfth-century Provence, Briffault's creative extravagance might have declared that the earth's conditions were perfect for human life. The air contained more oxygen than it does now; solar rays of a carcinogenic nature were arrested by an immaculate atmosphere. Pure glacial river water was refined in pink fish, and every grain and fruit was uncontaminated. The Provençal language, vernacular yet literate, shaped itself to the service of the sensibility of its poetry. It harbored the shades and subtleties necessary for the expression of the means and vagaries of the heart in love. It brought metaphor to a sublime level of perfection, and at the same time it contradicted the declamations of pope or savage. We may infer that, by contrast, the contemporary world is befouled, poisoned, psychotic, deluded, and bellicose; that cyber-mediation has erected a comprehensive counterfeiture, and that monkey-men have willingly forfeited their power of discretion. Persons may now meekly detect within themselves an echo of privacy, but very little remains of the constructs of the natural man, the noble savage, or the free man. In Provence peripatetic troubadours wandered, foraged for food, and daydreamed under a tree. They were unmediated, and reposed in a blessed state of personal privacy. We may wish, dearly, to sympathize with that bucolic scene, but the war is real within us every day we dare to consider how we may have gotten our religions and philosophies to a place in which we easily tolerate the fact that billions of persons starve while a few others thrive. A significant part of that process has been accepting that war is the natural condition of man.

At Passchendaele the mud was oceanic. The fearsome might of the mud penetrated virtually everything. Horseshit and mud have been mostly detached from the modern consciousness, as has the certain fatality of septic wounds. Many men went mad, and yet millions of others did not. And it is the palsying shell shock, paradoxically, by which we may begin to enter the mental world of the soldier in the trench. Its effects included uncontrollable trembling and contortions, blinding rages, catatonia, and a range of other mental and physical debilities. The affliction resembles the modern malaises centered around anomie, depression, or having been made superfluous. Walker Percy wrote: "The only treatment for angelism, that is, excessive abstraction of the self from itself, is recovery of the self through ordeal." It was not exactly time that stood still just before departing a trench and lurching toward odds favorable to death or gruesome wound, for those moments were about one kind of moment before another one. Duration was a tense that had suddenly lost all meaning, as past, present, and future melded together.

Manning:

> One had a vague feeling that one was going away, without any notion of returning. One had finished with the place, and did not regret it; but a curious instability of mind accompanied the last moments: with a sense of actual relief that the inexorable hour was approaching, there was a growing anger becoming so intense that it seemed the heart would scarcely hold it. The skin seemed shinier and tighter on men's faces, and eyes burned with a hard brightness under the brims of their helmets. One felt every question as an interruption of some absorbing business of the mind. One by one, they realized that each must go alone, and that each of them already was alone with himself, helping others perhaps, but looking at them with strange eyes, while the world became unreal and empty, and they moved in a mystery, where no help was.

They did not, always, quite name this "fear." They did not necessarily feel more attached to the precious bright gift of life in moments that seemed to have with death an overwhelming reciprocity. Narrowed and hollow irises were not glimpsing existentialism, or some form of blood or belief; they were simply one man's *story* for the moment altogether sublimated, its atoms transformed into an undefiled and undifferentiated consciousness.

For every soldier, the battlefield was a place of his own making. While the war was the ultimate expression of the extent to which rule-following can remove a personality from his or her own autonomy, within his mind, he was alone. The mysteries and irresolutions of life are formless and eternal until one locates a moment where they are not—that split-time of present, lacking a past, absent of a future, where no equivocation was possible.

Certainly Tommy and Fritz did not trouble themselves with trying to sort out why the war was being fought. As they were subjected to threats and propaganda, they could not have remained insensitive to the allegations that the enemy might soon mutilate their family. Indeed atrocities had been committed upon the people of what was commonly called "Gallant Little Belgium," and political nuance was because of that absent. The knowledge that nations were aggressively arming themselves well prior to 1914 formed a base momentum, metastasizing from which were governmental misinterpretation and mismanagement, nationalistic paranoia, economic interests in the form of securing markets and protecting resources (not least oil), and the feeble psychologies associated with perceived threat and actual bullying. These conditions helped promote the context from which war enthusiasm grew, and out of which massive and enthusiastic armies could be raised. That context was extinguished in the trenches, when a man faced a gun that was inspired to shoot principally, or only because it was being threatened by another gun. Time and self vanished; afterwards, if they survived, time and self might recrudesce slowly, but men might never again understand humankind in quite the same way.

Llewelyn Wyn Griffith of the Royal Welch Fusiliers wrote:

> It was life rather than death that faded away into the distance, as I grew into a state of not-thinking, not-feeling, not-seeing. I moved past trees, past other things; men passed by me, carrying other men, some crying, some cursing, some silent. They were all shadows, and I was no greater than they. Living or dead, all were unreal. Past and future were equidistant and unattainable, throwing no bridge of desire across the gap that separated me from my remembered self and from all that I had hoped to grasp. I walked as on a mountain in a

mist, seeing neither sky above nor valley beneath, lost to all sense of
far or near, up or down, either in time or space. I saw no precipice,
and so I feared none.

Soldiers did not always exhibit courage, though sometimes their
impulses and actions of brave excess resembled the thing that we call
courage. Gallantry, often used to describe the acts of men at the front,
was doubtless a word never used by men committing those acts. Their
actions were more the desperation of a deep craving to just keep breathing; more it was fear of collegial cowardice. It was not a *different* character that sprung from docile shopkeepers when they found themselves
launching themselves into preposterous and suicidal acts of selfless
abandon to save a man they did not know. It might be thought of as
the shucking away of the crusts that ages of covetousness and greed had
left on them. Culture, for Briffault, was a teeming roil of combinant
and rival forces. It was the final admixture of the civility of man and
the elemental nerves of the caveman for whom the difference between
murder and survival was indistinguishable. Here thousands of rats over-
ran men's temporary dens, and proved their superiority. Things were
not making sense. Strange extrapolation became normal. *An Oxonian
ventured to read* Hamlet *in the cess-cistern trenches of the lowlands, his mind
was sacking Rome. The Catalunyan Usatges anteceded the Magna Carta by
a hundred years. For Cervantes tauromachia was at once blood sport and fine
art. Celts and gnomes riverrun. "Watch Spain."* Were the rumors true, that
late in the war, Germans wired three corpses together for rendering in
vats (and was that for armament or food?). Comprehensive confusion
degenerated into madness and moral pain.

Artillery shells would land a foot from a man and no trace of him could
be found, for the incendiary explosion liquefied his soul and bones.
Another shell could land a few inches from a man, and it would not
affect or disarrange his uniform or skin; but he too would be dead.
Some Australians would stroll insouciant through a rain of shells, and
would charge trenches by which they were numerically overmatched.

They might have done the same had they been unpaid, for the ANZACS were often rather a blunt sort. At the end of the war, packs of Aussie deserters menaced Belgian towns for food and plunder. One hundred thousand colonial Indian troops formed the fiercest corps; their penchant for beheading enemy soldiers was no rumor. Histories mention deserters, malingerers, and those who turned from the front and raced back to a familiar sort of safety—the trench they had just departed—only to be later court martialed and sometimes executed for desertion. Yet there were many thousands of English and German lads whose will, usually in a flash, continued with the charge, or who sacrificed their lives to protect their fellows. In London and Berlin, tremendous fortunes were made by businessmen who, sleeping, had scuttle across their face no rat.

In all the land armies of the war, a common phenomenon was remarked in memoirs and narrative accounts: in a shell hole, mortally imperiled, surely to be maimed or killed, soldiers were visited by a whelming sensation of apathy or indifference. This has been reported as a sublime disaffection; one might say they were cool. That state of mind will have been preceded by grotesque assaults upon whatever balance of soul and mind a soldier might have possessed: thunderous concussive blows to the ear, a sky filled with fire, and much pre-evidence of one's own homicide. It was a compelling and absolute medium, and minds dissolved. Captured soldiers were always complacent and cooperative with their captors, at times cordial, and even affectionate, conceivably due to the fact that more than that their war was over, the madness was over. Medics habituated themselves to seeing skin turned inside out and organs leathered by fire. For many soldiers, disillusion with the forged rationale of the war and inurement to observing gruesome deaths proceeded at roughly the same rate, usually resulting in benumbed reason and callused emotions. This accompanied the obscure wants of vitamin deficiency, the deterioration of resistance, and the aggregating woes of the dispiriting constancy of wet, cold, and lice. Stanley Dell, a Princetonian serving with the French Ambulance Service, reassured Edmund Wilson con-

cerning the latter's fear of being unable to withstand the constant exposure to death if he were to join the corps. Dell wrote Wilson: "nothing
gets exhausted so quickly as human sympathy."

During a desultory, almost lazy bombardment, Jack and George are in
conversation. George is reading a letter from his new wife Bets describing her work in a munitions factory, where she spends ten hours a day
six days a week assembling a small portion of an interior mechanism
she has been told relates to a preliminary function of the "enactor,"
but a small, broken section of a child's sled runner that has been
packed into an explosive device—assembled by another wife in farmland near Stuttgart—creates a severe shrill no one close by can hear,
when, now as a piece of shrapnel at a thousand miles an hour ripping
into George's face, halving the cranial compartment and flinging
wet bits of brain into Jack's nostrils, it becomes a supercharged injection which creates an immediate involuntary sneeze, as other parts
of the oblongata sting his cheek, and which, much later and forever,
he will regard as the electro-chemical action that was George's vision
of Bets, as he read her letter about her having just finished her breakfast, which was reminding him of her endearing way of buttering toast.

The whole of the Great War, 1914-1918, was a malicious demonstra-
tion of how far civilized societies could venture from reason, common-
weal, justice, decency, and mental health. Survivors unaffected by
the collective, intentional amnesia that normally follows war have
conjectured what this particular war-disease might have been for. A
comrade was killed an arm's length distant, in the middle of a
conversation. Where is his response to the question we were asking him?
Outgoing letters are in censors' hands written by soldiers that morning
killed—where does the sentiment go? A man saves your life at noon,
and he is dead by dusk: whither one's thanks so dear? When trauma
grafts onto the breath and blood, how can it ever fade away? Yet it
did fade for most men. British foot soldiers returned to their lot in

life, German soldiers returned to militarism, and politicians regenerated the nationalistic delusions and psychoses that had led to a war horribly called Great.

iii.

THE GHOSTS' BIBLIOGRAPHY

The first published writing about the war was 1916's *Le Feu*, released as *Under Fire*, by Henri Barbusse, a French soldier. It is a poetic, prismatic impression of his battlefield experience. He presents the battle scene as a mosaic of elements. Blasts of blinding light and retorts of reverberation wash over the man in the trench, a pointillism for which no soldier had ever been prepared. Barbusse was later turned by the war to Bolshevik communism, and his writing makes it possible to suppose that communism is the single best dialectic by which one can ever begin to comprehend "war for war's sake," which is what the Great War indeed became as the trenches were first dug. For when the original stakes were rendered irrelevant, the war was fought only to win the war that had been started. Very few of the participants in the war (excluding the journalists) placed themselves in an observational historical context, yet the soldier poet Siegfried Sassoon and the writer Wyndham Lewis read Barbusse's book while serving in the trenches in 1917, an effect that might have done queer things to their sense of observation, description, and literary discourse. Barbusse was the first published writer who had written about the war never having read a printed word about it.

Le Feu also influenced Abel Gance, whose 1919 silent movie *J'Accuse* was partly filmed at the battle at Saint-Mihiel in 1918. The movie is virulently anti-war, and does not soften the viciousness of the butchery, rapes, and insanity. The end of the movie features two thousand soldiers in a macabre tableau known as "the return of the dead." Gance recalled:

> The conditions in which we filmed were profoundly moving. . . . These men had come straight from the Front—from Verdun—and they were due back eight days later. They played the dead knowing that in all probability they'd be dead themselves before long. Within a few weeks of their return, eighty per cent had been killed.

An even earlier film, 1916's *Joan of Arc of Loos*, by the Australian Franklyn Barrett is based on Émilienne Moreau-Evrard's heroic acts of inspiration and sacrifice, and depicts German atrocities in France in 1915. The film was frequently used for propaganda purposes. In 1930 G.W. Pabst directed *Westfront 1918*, an expression of the New Objectivity and its directness relating to social subjects and conditions. The film follows a small group of soldiers in the German Army through their demoralization and to their deaths. Correctly understood as a pacifist denunciation of war, the movie was suppressed during the Third Reich. Also suppressed was Ernst Lubitsch's 1932 pacifist film *Broken Lullaby*, in which a French soldier comes to realize that the German soldier he has killed in the war was, like himself, a musician. His efforts to atone to the German's family are rebuffed until he is accompanied on piano by the late soldier's widow.

Frank Herbert Simonds also begins his traditional history of the conflict *in medias res*, publishing Volume I of his multi-volume *History of the World War* in 1917, as the war is "entering its thirty-fourth month." With no certainty about how the war will end, no more unprejudiced description is possible. Simonds does not evaluate the war culturally, and presents the conflict only as a series of skirmishes and retreats, the establishment of trenches, and battles, all without historical context.

Arthur Guy Empey's *Over the Top* was published in 1917, one of the first popular stories heard from the front, and the book was commercially very successful. Firmly set in the voice of its times, expressing a view both dry and hearty, a young American from Jersey City had contrived his way into the British Expeditionary Force, served in the field, and was wounded at the Somme. Empey was a sanguine and brisk fellow who in later life became a pulp novelist, writer of screenplays, and a B-film producer. Bert Hall's 1918 book *En l'air!*, exaggerates his own not-always-noble exploits during his troubled pass through the Lafayette Escadrille, the band of American flyers serving with the French Air Corps prior to America's entry in the war in 1917.

Rebecca West's 1918 novel *The Return of the Soldier* is concerned chiefly with the shell-shock of a British officer, and his struggle while seeking readjustment and treatment in England. His cousin Jenny's construal of the trauma provides one the first accounts of the war from the homeland, from a non-combatant, and from a woman. Colette's 1919 novella *Mitsou* considers the war from the perspective of a young Parisian showgirl, who has met a lieutenant on leave. His letters to her reveal Colette's characteristic insight into the war's effect on manhood, and the relationships between returning soldiers and women. He writes to her having returned to the front:

> Dear, dear Mitsou, how I like everything about you, and especially how anxiously your letters describe for me your clean and sad life, as empty as a new attic! Do you know mine is almost as empty? Mitsou, we boys of twenty four, the war grabbed us just as we came out of college. It made us into men, and I am afraid that we shall never recover from having missed the time of growing up. We lost forever that precious period, in which we might have learnt poise and balance in voice and manner, and the habit of being free, and how to treat our families and how to approach women without being afraid or acting like cannibals—women, I mean, who would not be thinking only of our desires or our money. Mitsou, forgive me for boring you with all this. The reason is that just now my regrets have a special reason: am I going to throw at your feet an overgrown schoolboy or a much-too-young grown man, who will be like a fruit out of season, ripe on one side and green on the other?

An unusual perspective on the war is presented in *Just behind the Front in France*, by Noble Foster Hoggson. Written in 1916 and published in

1918, Hoggson was a member of the American Industrial Commission to France, examining the effects of the first two years of the war on the region's infrastructure. In the course of his technical tasks, Hoggson makes several acute and humane observations. Never ignoring the horrible loss of life, he notes that French citizens, though almost all are living in the cellars of destroyed homes and churches, are already accumulating bits of material from the armaments and associated equipment to save for sale to the battlefield and cemetery tourists they know will come with the end of the war. It was a bit of speculative commerce that was indeed fulfilled. This was not the only planning: Hoggson reports on the French *Comprehensive Plan for Reforestation*, and the country's systematic accrual of justifications—bullet points—for an inevitable Reconstruction Bill. Replacement benefits, in fact, were already being distributed in 1916, and displaced persons' accommodations were the subject of much invidious discussion behind the front. Hoggson observes the temporary burial trenches and graves, which created what he referred to as a "democracy of the dead," in which distinctions of class, race, and rank were absent. Vast numbers of the aristocracy were killed, having responded to their call of noble duty. The rate of death for British junior officers was actually greater than for the trench soldier. Hoggson pays both professional and personal attention to the many cathedrals that were destroyed, particularly the magnificent one at Reims, site of the coronation of several French kings. Reims Cathedral had minimal strategic value for the Germans. Its destruction had more to do with the extinguishment of cultural sites, among which the ruination of Louvain's precious library was the prime example. Hoggson calls the war "a holocaust."

> With painful forebodings I approached the great cathedral. I dreaded to see what I had already learned—that it was damaged beyond repair. From a little distance the exterior damage did not seem serious, but on close inspection the real results of the abominable crime were laid bare. The upper roof had been completely burned off but the vaulted stone roof, though pierced here and there by gaping shell-holes, remained intact and apparently in good condition. A feeling of deep depression possessed me as I walked down

the nave of this once noble church, now desecrated by men who
claim the pinnacle of culture. In its melancholy ruin it seemed like
the corpse of a great evangel whose soul had departed. Numerous
pigeons were wheeling in and out through the glassless windows and
circling about in the remote shadows of the arched stone ceiling one
hundred and twenty feet above the eye.

Contemporary and later accounts frequently describe the bitter juxtaposition of the profound and the ridiculous, on occasion taking the form
of an officer filling out forms in triplicate regarding cutlery or cloth
hats three hours after his platoon has been wiped out. Hoggson, like
other commentators, is amazed by the fantastic efficiency of the post
trains, such that that a letter scrawled in a trench would arrive surely in
Edinburgh three days later, so committed was the army to maintaining
the correspondence of its soldiers (while still suppressing substantive
information). Hoggson reports on ancillary activities in France: Sister
Julie of the Hospice of Saint Charles achieved great fame for upbraid-
ing a German officer who presumed to harm the wounded in her care.
Though the Germans had butchered sixty women and children and left
their bodies in the streets of Gerbevillier, Sister Julie was also caring for
wounded German soldiers, wanting only to prevent more death. The
California Committee for Reconstruction had specified the village of
Vitrimont for its assistance. The funds raised in America were adminis-
tered in France by Miss Daisy Polk of San Francisco, who employed fifty
men unfit for combat to repair and rebuild roofs and walls. Hoggson's
accounts read with the vividness of a newsreel, and perhaps no com-
mentator has more effectively described the damage and scars that were
inflicted upon the pacific meadows and gentle towns of eastern France.

The English poet Edmund Blunden's 1928 *Undertones of War* remains a
persuasive example of recollections of the war in which a poetic telling
(and titling) convey the unknowable "otherness" of those internecine
killing fields. Appended to his narrative are several of his poems. The
allusive and metaphorical verses are illuminating and provide direct
transport to a place about which we never had any knowledge, and for

which we never had preparation. Blunden understands the war as purely the work of the minds of men, recounting the atrocities and the shame through a massive weave of syntax, rhetoric, metaphor, deep semantics, and the lyric verse that still remains the vestigial heart of English prose. After the war Blunden lived and taught in Tokyo, his mind on the Japanese language's ideograms, fossils, and visual conjugations. We might too speculate that Blunden would provide us with the least sentimental or clichéd descriptions of the rosy fingers of dawn diffusing themselves over the littering corpses, but in fact most accounts, by souls from Saskatchewan or Silesia, include unexpectedly expressive descriptions of the scenes, often employing words that surprise us until they are understood not only as sincere, but as the only ones that will possibly do. In dreams and books we close the gap between our sofa chair with coffee and the absolute horror of the trenches. The eye Blunden cast upon the broad scene was both poetic and journalistic; trained to discretion and literary criticism, and as such he possessed a necessary impartiality as he watched the fevered looting of corpses. This ubiquitous robbing, he learned, had distinguishable parts: for souveniering, for food or cigarettes, or for additional instruments of killing. The linguist Blunden mentions that sprees of artillery were sometimes called "hates." In the gloomy fields of bleak weather and dark thoughts, an accentuated despair attached itself to the raids called for by distantly removed event planners. In these night guerrilla attacks, five or six men would prowl across No Man's Land to invade an enemy trench, there to bayonet the throats, eyes, and abdomens of their kind. The goal of the activity was to instill terror, or to learn of conditions, and often to capture an individual of other-clothed persuasion for the extraction of useful military information.

Many memoirs from the Great War describe the backvillage *estaminets*, where life's principal elements existed with little apparent moderation: sustenance, calmatives, brotherhood, the removal of inhibitions, and the particular disport of madness and merriment that leads to the perpetuation of the species. Its agents were roasted chickens, American cigarettes, hale fellows singing all together, whiskey and beer, and young mademoiselles and *missen* carrying out their eternal mission-work of *ewig weibliche*. Blunden characterizes personalities who seem to be unchanged by the environment: men who find a true kind word for the dying, and who are not unduly dispirited by the inevitability of their platoons being mercilessly halved. We hear examples of precious, intimate conversations of men hovering at the precipice of non-existence. Such words were whispered across all the battle fronts in something of a choral woe. And Blunden evokes the ghostly power of naming the name, for Doogan and Worley, Jones, and Hobson die, while thousands upon thousands of other deaths are unremarked, and attract to themselves no drama at all, though they bear names too. Attempting to ameliorate the terrors brought on by imminent danger and the confusions of being, many soldiers read books, Oxbridge scholars frequently choosing Greek philosophers or medieval philosophers. Blunden writes from Zillebeke and Ypres, amid especially vicious bombardments:

> During this period my indebtedness to an eighteenth-century poet became enormous. At every spare moment I read in Young's *Night Thoughts on Life, Death and Immortality*, and I felt the benefit of this grave and intellectual voice, speaking out of a profound eighteenth-century calm, often in metaphor which came home to one even in a pillbox. The mere amusement of discovering lines applicable to our crisis kept me from despair.

The War the Infantry Knew by James Churchill Dunn, a British Expeditionary Force Medical Officer, had a curious publishing history and a fusional composition that effectively if inadvertently replicates the multi-vectored crescendos of the battles of the Great War. After an anonymous private publication in 1938, the book faded away, to be resurrected and achieve proper attribution only in 1987. Dunn refers to himself very rarely, and then only in the third person, but the text is a seamless aggregation of diaries and letters from several other officers and soldiers of the Royal Welch Fusiliers, (the idiomatic spelling proudly retained), which blend and shift from one to another without obvious citation. The result is an amalgam of tones of voice, a Rashomon of opinions and observations about discrete events and the whole of the experience.

The book's prose is curious and interesting, the sort of especially compelling writing that exhibits lucidity, force, and ease (the paramount rules of prose set down by Edmund Wilson) by persons who are not, first, writers, but whose other sorts of training may create equally exact analysis and expression. With the dryness that is associated with Brits in a spot, Dunn notes how communications from the front indicate that "the situation is obscure." Inquiries about botched actions find that "no one who matters is to blame," and "operations were farcical from the beginning."

> Next we learned by telephone that there was to be no release yet from the caprice of the abstract tactician who from far-away disposes of us: someone playing fantastic tricks with reality had substituted 30 seconds shooting by two unregistered trench-mortars for the impotent batteries of guns. This was confirmed in an amended Brigade Operation Order, spread over an extra half-sheet of paper. There are times when foolscap is fitting, and ironic mirth is a safety-valve.

Other comical and lethal forays are attributed to "some dilettante at a seaside resort, fresh from a gay time in Paris, [who] is supposed to have devised the scheme." (Such insouciance led specifically to the miseries and decimation of the American Lost Battalion in 1918.) Griping about leaders' bull-headed tactical mistakes can be assumed for the foot soldiers of every armed force, though in the First World War, the remoteness of the soldiers from officers resulted in sacrifices that might be considered a blithe disconcern.

The book records telling details of observation: "A bad blister on a man's heel might be the only thing he could clearly remember after a week of intense experience which added a battle honour to the colors of his regiment." The rats, "made a noise like wind through corn." Late in the war, Yankees are welcomed, and not much liked. Most volunteers for lethal raids and other deadly tasks are the older

men, which was the case too in the German military forces. Dunn
supposes that this is because older men have been already "disillu-
sioned by life." He stresses the point too that thousands of men were
sent into hopeless situations by "cavalry generals," who were slow
to understand trench attrition, having been trained in the regular
army, which could only imagine grand Napoleonic battles of movement. A typical obfuscation was the use of "accessories," by which
was meant gas, and its inevitable grotesque asphyxiations, which
some officers tried to prevent their men from seeing. Local citizens
included quite a number of spies for the Germans, and one very
young local girl ventured into the trenches to sell chocolates. Dunn
"doubts if the men here are more drawn to religion; I'm sure they are
more than ever repelled by the clergy." Finally, he writes with some
considerable sadness observing, towards the end of the war, the
collapse of morale among the German soldiers; their complicit
surrenders, their emaciation, extreme youth, and spiritual desolation. The war was not won by Allied British Forces; it came to
its pathetic end simply because the Germans could no longer mount
fighting forces.

It is useful to recall the pace and scope of lives that were interrupted or
truncated by the war, and Siegfried Sassoon's *The Complete Memoirs of
George Sherston* contextualizes the social disorder occasioned by that
ugliest of disruptions. American readers may have some difficulty
divorcing the sophisticated cunning and beauty of fox hunting
from its foul redolence of privilege and farmfield-trampling arrogance, but Sassoon's first section "Memoirs of a Fox-Hunting Man"
well expresses the injury that was done to the famously sunny and
blissful summer of 1914. Sassoon's loving devotion to fox hunting
and cricket enhances his description of the world in which such
hours of equanimity and peace of mind were tortured into years
of anguish and sorrow. Close relationships with grooms are deeply
appreciated as more than a function of service, when a dedicated

horseman of the subservient class, Dixon, is killed to an equal measure of sorrow as Sherston's fellow Cambridge University officers. Though awful numbers of both social sets were killed, the typical resolution and fortitude of the common soldiers in the trenches—men who perhaps had much less to hope for if the war were to end favorably for the Commonwealth—can seem a dearer gift of natural generosity. Sassoon writes: "Courage remained a virtue. And that exploitation of courage, if I may be allowed to say a thing so obvious, was the essential tragedy of the War, which, as everyone now agrees, was a crime against humanity." The techniques of this particular war, noted frequently in the literature—the trench, the parapet, the loopholes in the sandbags—occasioned, more often than one would think possible, a black spot to appear with shocking suddenness slightly above and between the eyebrows, in the midst of a conversation, during the exhalation of a laugh, to be followed by the appearance at another's feet a one hundred and forty pound, and utterly motionless, corpse, your fellow. The British poet Charles Sorley was killed in just this way, at the Battle of Loos. The entirely unprejudiced way in which Sassoon places a report of an instance of this effect into a graceful bit of prose English conveys across the years the depraved randomness of death. The war in all ways, was, for the author, "that big bullying bogey." Watching an exhausted Division return from the Somme offensive, he thinks he "had watched an army of ghosts. It was as though I had seen the War as it might be envisioned by the mind of some epic poet a hundred years hence."

Sassoon died in 1967, after an exceptional life of scholarship and unconventionality. His service in the Army amounted to a series of astounding exploits and repeated episodes of bravery that often struck his men as crazier than courageous. Sassoon's war comes down to us as a writer's war. Though now less appreciated for his contributions to literature, we read his account through the elucidation that mark a writer's craft. There is evident care not to ambush his readers with a dazzle of narrative, but to present a kind of whole field. Home in England on leave, he receives a letter from a comrade at the front, reporting that "Edmunds was killed, and Asbestos Bill died of his wounds, Fernby was not expected to live, Miles and Danby both killed." He puts the letter down:

> I walked about the room, whistling and putting the pictures straight. Then a gong rang for luncheon. Aunt Evelyn drew my attention to the figs, which were the best we'd had off the old tree that autumn.

Incipient doubts about the nature of the political aims of the war eventually overruled his sense of duty, and Sassoon published *Finished with the War: A Soldier's Declaration*, in July of 1917.

> I am making this statement as an act of willful defiance of military authority, because I believe that the War is being deliberately prolonged by those who have the power to end it. I am a soldier, convinced that I am acting on behalf of soldiers. I believe this War, upon which I entered as a war of defence and liberation, has now become a war of aggression and conquest. I believe that the purposes for which I and my fellow-soldiers entered upon this War should have been so clearly stated as to have made it impossible for them to be changed without our knowledge, and that, had this been done, the objects which actuated us would now be attainable by negotiation. I have seen and endured the sufferings of the troops, and I can no longer be a party to prolonging those sufferings for ends which I believe to be evil and unjust. I am not protesting against the military conduct of the War, but against the political errors and insincerities for which the fighting men are being sacrificed. On behalf of those who are suffering now, I make this protest against the deception which is being practiced on them. Also I believe that it may help to destroy the callous complacence with which the majority of those at home regard the continuance of agonies which they do not share, and which they have not sufficient imagination to realise.

Sassoon was sent to Craiglockhart Hospital in Scotland, nominally for shell-shock, but chiefly to remove him from public view. After conversations with the revered psychiatrist W.H.R. Rivers, and out of a tangle of reconsiderations and reevaluations, he eventually recanted his objection, and re-entered the service. An account of his hospitalization and evolving therapeutic reasoning appears in the *Regeneration* trilogy of novels by Pat Barker.

Speaking, in part, of shell-shock, Sassoon concludes that the war's victims'

> humanity had been outraged by those explosives which were sanctioned and glorified by the Churches; it was thus that their self-sacrifice was mocked and maltreated—they, who in the name of righteousness had been sent out to maim and slaughter their fellow-men. In the name of civilization these soldiers had been martyred, and it remained for civilization to prove that their martyrdom wasn't a dirty swindle.

Thousands of British crosses in France and Flanders signified that capitalism was protected, profits were accrued, and the empire was saved. But the specifically enclosed location of such remembrances implied that upon leaving the cemetery, forgetting it all was permitted, and even possible.

The American Marine Elton Mackin's diaries were first published eighty years after they were written. His experiences provide a full view of 1918, the year in which the war degenerated to its pathetic conclusion. He is not known to have written anything else in his life, depriving readers and historians of a keen observer, for his recreation of the dialogues of his fellow-soldiers bears the authenticity of a transcript. Many plays and books have been titled from Shakespeare's plays and poems, but this conceit does not appear ever to have influenced Mackin or his publisher, for the title of his book—though one may quibble with the semantics—presents the reader the droll essence of concision and blunt force: *Suddenly We Didn't Want to Die*. Another expression of this sentiment appeared in Richard Suskind's 1964 Bantam pulp fictionalization of the Americans' 1918 resistance to the last German offensive at Belleau Wood. It was titled *Do You Want to Live Forever!*

The arching matter of Wyndham Lewis' 1937 autobiography *Blasting and Bombardiering* is its strict and perhaps even diabolical maintenance of a wry tone. For the pre-eminent Vorticist of his times, it was vital that he maintain a rigid superiority of such haughtiness of mind that even the memory of a thousand exploded bodies could not interfere with his authorial nobility. But as an essayist and artist, Lewis has considerable value in illuminating the truth that folly is actually a form of madness, in the face of which a rancorous grimace may be most apt. Though Blunden's prose can be considered the most euphonious (and therefore metaphysical) to come out of the war, it is Lewis' Vorticist prose that might be considered the most appropriate, with its faceted planes, serrations, and severe exteriority. As Lewis has his character Tarr remark, "Art has no inside, nothing you cannot see."

> The preparations for Passchendaele were a poem in mud cum blood-and-thunder. The appetite of the Teuton for this odd game called war—in which a dum-dum bullet is a foul, but a gas-bomb is okay—and British 'doggedness' in the gentle art of 'muddling through,' when other nations misunderstood British kindliness and get tough, made a perfect combination. If the Germans and English had not been there, all the others would long before that have run away and the war been over. These two contrasted but as it were complementary types of idée fixe found their perfect expression on the battlefield, or battle-bog, of Passchendaele. The very name, with its suggestion of splashiness and passion at once, was subtly appropriate. This nonsense could not have come to its full flower at any other place but at Passchendaele. It was pre-ordained. The moment I saw the name on the trench-map, intuitively I knew what was going to happen.

Lewis first served as a second lieutenant in the Royal Artillery, chiefly in the exceptionally perilous role as a forward observer. After his service at Passchendaele, he was appointed an official war artist. His modernist paintings, *A Canadian Gun-Pit* (at Vimy Ridge), and *A Battery Shelled*, may have surprised a citizenry accustomed to more practical and heroic depictions of the battlefront, but each has become a notable expression of the intersection of Modernist art and the grotesqueries occasioned by the war. Such contradictions are suggested too by the titles of Lewis' novels, among them *Monstre Gai, Malign Fiesta, Rotting Hill, The Revenge for Love, The Roaring Queen,* and *Filibusters in Barbary.*

Lewis' letters from war-stricken France and Belgium more often concern his seeking publication of his writings or exhibitions of his artwork; they also illustrate his colorful battles with colleagues, critics and foes. He wrote Mary Borden in the summer of 1915:

> I must join the Army. I have as little reason to be shot at once and *without a hearsay* as any artist in Europe, but have certain accomplishments (such as an unusual mastery of French) that might be of more use to pen-polyglots alliés than my trusty right arm, which, I flatter myself, is rather a creative than a destructive limb. I understand that interpreters get shot *at once:* that 80 percent already lie dead. A 2nd lieut.'s commission in the infantry is a death warrant more or less.

He wrote Ezra Pound, having enjoyed reading Barbusse's *Le Feu,* and mentioned that "we were shelled and gassed all night. I had my respirator on for two solid hours."

Another often-neglected aspect of the war and life lived in trenches, dugouts, billets, and bunkers concerns the human relations necessitated by the artificial social organizations. Lewis again, writing to Pound:

> I think I told you we had a new C.O. He comes from Hull, from its Slums undoubtedly, and its Sunday Schools. The proud Naval man to whom were were attached would hardly speak to him, and wondered once more at the ways of the Army, in giving such an unspeakable and foolish [man] a Battery.
>
> We have to do a lot of forward observation. Ainsi, I was F.O.O. (forward ob officer) of the Group three days ago, and on that occasion had the extreme gratification of seeing, in the midst of our barrage, a large Bosche fly into the air, as it seemed a few feet beneath me. From the ridge where I was observing things I looked down into the German front line as you might into Church Street.

In a 1950 piece of autobiographical writing, *Rude Assignment*, he contemplated the primary disease of the twentieth century:

> On the battlefield of France and Flanders I became curious about how and why these bloodbaths occurred—the political mechanics of war. I acquired a knowledge of some of the intricacies of the power-game, the usurious economics associated with war-making.

In *The Revenge for Love* Lewis had ridiculed and abjured the Republican Spanish Civil War, and secured his friends' enmity by being too late (1939) in repudiating Hitler. Wyndham Lewis was one of the most oppositional dogmatics to come out of the war, and his anti-liberal rancor can always seem staged or rhetorical. But like countless citizens in England and Germany and their affiliated nation-states, the war proved to be a moment that might, or must contradict their personal assurances of pacifism or otherness: they joined the Army.

After Sassoon's memoirs, Robert Graves' *Goodbye to All That* is perhaps the most referenced book about the First World War by its participants. Graves' writing lacks a certain humility; perhaps his perimeters are too sharp, too clean. It is true that Graves' expression of disillusionment has the most literary resonance, and in this way his record of the war's futility and the warmakers' hubris will last indefinitely. But he allows readers to infer that his bitterness and his disillusion are more royal than, say, rough Empey's. Sassoon and Blunden deplored Graves' book, mostly on matters of fact, but their disfavor is also an expression of their rejection of his sterile intellectualization of the blood in the mud.

Vera Brittain left Somerville College Oxford University to become a nurse with the Voluntary Aid Detachment, and served in France and Malta. She later wrote of her war experiences in *Testament of Youth* (1933), and hers are among the richest descriptions we have of the moment of death, with its metaphysical anomie and wonder. The war for her is the single soldier, the citizen of England, abused. Early in the book Brittain writes about the girls in England's schools, "which sterilized the sexual charm out of their pupils and turned them into hockey-playing hoydens with gauche manners and an armoury of inhibitions," but she may as well have been speaking of the callow youth who became soldiers. By 1918, the war has killed her fiancé, her brother, and two close friends; she has become a militant feminist and pacifist, and she is thereafter closest with the writer Winifred Holtby (separately chronicled in *Testament of a Friendship*). England and the English war have wounded her deeply, and turned a life that might have been a thousand flowers blooming into one of pure resistance against depression and the surrender of her will. The war years are for her a span of fluctuating spirits and faked morale; moreover, they are speckled with telegrams arriving at otherwise undistinguished moments announcing that another has been killed, later, another, and after a while, another. "There is something so starved and dry about hospital nurses—as if they had to force all the warmth out of themselves before they could be really good nurses," Brittain writes. They are prohibited from telling wounded soldiers their names. She speaks of her several moments of contemplation and grief: "I went up Denmark Hill to try to think out in solitude all the implications of my spasmodic angers, my furious, uncontrolled resentments." Brittain prevails, always prevails, but her days are ceaselessly flavored with suffering and melancholy. Even at a more sublime level, she reads the darker truth of the forces that encourages persons to abet the forces that militate against their own interests:

> Between 1914 and 1918 young men and women, disastrously pure in heart and unsuspicious of elderly self-interest and cynical exploitation, were continually rededicating themselves to an end that they believed, and went on trying to believe, lofty and ideal. [I wanted to] know why it had been possible for me and my contemporaries, through our own ignorance and others' ingenuity, to be used, hypnotised and slaughtered.

It is Vera Brittain's percipience that sees most clearly that thousands of survivors are going to return to England's menial world, and dissipate the strength of soul that had been forged and enriched in Flanders fields. It is poetry by which she strives to refresh herself, when she has been bled pale by the interminable weight of her depressions, but she never seems to find the personal idiom necessary to finally extract the blackness from her spirit.

Vera Brittain is among those—and it is no small number, though perhaps obscured by the pictorially more satisfying scenes attending the news of the Armistice—for whom the end of the war and its unspeakable brutality was no occasion for celebration; instead it was a moment to realize that millions of persons were forever lost, and that other souls had been driven toward bestiality for no good reason. After the war, Brittain observes that veterans are discredited, and they are themselves drafted into a nation's enforced amnesia:

> No doubt the post-war generation was wise in its assumption that patriotism had 'nothing to it,' and we pre-war lot were just poor boobs for letting ourselves be kidded into thinking that it had. The smashing up of one's youth seemed rather a heavy price to pay for making the mistake, but fools always did come in for more punishment than knaves; we knew that now.

Life after wartime cannot have the force of war's sinister horror, but it had its own kind of anemia, and its own loss of fortune.[4]

Lady Dorothie Feilding [so-spelled] (a descendant of the *Tom Jones* novelist Henry Fielding) also left behind an aristocratic and comfortable life in England to drive an ambulance in Flanders. She was the first woman to receive medals for bravery for her service so close to the explosions at the front. She became an English folk hero in her own time for her service in Belgium. Her recollections have been recently published as *Lady under Fire on the Western Front: the Great War Letters of Lady Dorothie Feilding*.

Edith Cavell was a British nurse serving in Belgium, arrested for harboring Allied soldiers and assisting their escape back to France. (She had also assisted German soldiers, and saved many of their lives.) She was executed by the German military, instantly becoming a noted heroine and propaganda figure. Edith Piaf, a child of France we may imagine unsullied by the war, born two months after the execution, is named after Nurse Cavell. The Belgian Red Cross worker Gabrielle Petit was a prolific underground and espionage worker, executed for spying by the Germans occupying Brussels.

In the tetralogy *Parade's End*, Ford Madox Ford's idiom is not Lewis's or Briffault's, though all three regarded the inherent corruption of the upper classes as the chief active ingredient in the poison of bad policies, decisions, and strategies that resulted in Britain's share of the responsibility for the war without winners, and left a crippled Europe inevitably bound by treaty to destroy itself a second time. It was said by the politicians that the moment the papers were signed in Compiègne, another war was assured in which Germany's grievance would be proclaimed. Ford was the master impressionist of the early modern writers; thus, in the tetralogy, details of the forces that have driven nations to war, and the machinations that carried it out are not always evident; instead, we are presented with the scenes of the effects, the impressions left behind by those forces. This allows a sort of aloofness from the bullets in the gut and the acrid gas in the throat, resulting in a contemporary and yet vaguely historical overview of the events, much like Sassoon's. This practice in Ford's novels suggests that unarticulated and unseen malignant forces inform everything that happens, and trying to attribute the war to arrogant generals or pugilistic national natures is to miss the point that it is an immanent decadence which has finally reigned. However it was not merely the sense or impressions of war that concerned Ford when he was soldiering with the Welch Regiment at the Somme, for there he was severely concussed, gassed, and experienced shell-shock.

The novels' structural crux resides in the person of young Valentine Wannop, a feminist and pacifist. As with Briffault, there are few natural antidotes to the war or to the forces that its entrenched clubmen so effectively promulgated, but Valentine's pure sense of shame and insult is among them. Her faith doubtless seemed vain and jejune to most people (and to contemporary readers of the novels) but her adherence to love and justice remains fully intact after the war.

We may gather from Ford that there was a fearsome intimacy in the moral and emotional intensities experienced by the soldiers. Men might have wondered how they could learn to watch men die, each death in its turn slightly less appalling, or at least each time slightly less unexpected. To that extent, we may suppose that men were writing their own emotional autobiographies, men for whom nothing of the sort—nothing so acutely personal—may have ever occurred. Christopher Tietjens (Ford's alter ego) stands with his own resolute Tory attitudes against the great societal shifts that will follow the war. As the work of an impressionist writer, these novels perhaps most convincingly suggest not only the deep penetration the war made into England and its spouses and bloodlines, but also the way in which it was regarded by too many persons only as a distant inconvenience.

In his 1929 novel *I Thought of Daisy*, Edmund Wilson describes the lives of literate men and women who existed directly or obliquely mindful of the searing memory of the war, in this case, in Greenwich Village in the early 1920s. Like Sassoon, Brittain, and many others, the subliminal existence of the shades of shell-shock are insinuated in the attitudes and actions Wilson appends to his characters. The book's protagonist has admired a somewhat older friend who had served in the ambulance corps, a character we may presume reflects Wilson's own experiential and moral fluctuations in the service:

> From Hugo's novel, then, it would appear that during the first months of his ambulance-driving, he was still sustained by his romantic faith and preoccupied with proving to himself his own capacity for endurance and courage. He tells us of the hero of his novel, that though most of the wounded men he had been carrying turned out to have died on the way, he had never felt so happy in his life as after successfully bringing his ambulance through the craters and geysers of a bombardment. At that time, after his first physical sinkings of nausea and fear, he had been able to line up corpses on the floor of the field hospital with less emotion

than he had once arranged books on the shelves of his bookcases at college, and he had incinerated amputated legs with less of real regret than he had once burnt discarded manuscripts.

The quandary facing survivors entailed their gauging the balance of the vivid enjoyment of life with the evidence that their cultural firmament had turned brutal and ugly. In the Village, Wilson's alter ego lives in the dense milieu of writers and artists, among egomaniacs, ponderous thinkers, and frauds. The book is 311 pages of the story's unfolding, reflections, and the scurryings of persons in the arts, but its deeper implications concern memory, and the process of memory (plot develops, but even more importantly, I *thought* of Daisy). Memory, in the form of paying one's dour respects, resembles the war monuments that provide the comforting illusion of sympathy and commiseration. But the only true account we will ever achieve requires some form of personal hypnotism, by which we assign our hearts and minds into the trenches, or imagine ourselves feeding limbs into the incinerator. Bitter cognitive empathy pales formal acts of commemoration.

> Since the War, the discussion of literature had affected him like his memories of college, and the spectre of the modern literary man, whom he had encountered at New York parties and Paris cafés, came to accompany, and to merge with, the spectre of the aesthetic undergraduate. Though he had in his youth been full of literary enthusiasms, he now habitually treated the great writers—including those whom he most admired, from Plato to James Joyce—in a manner cavalier almost to the point of hysteria. It was partly, I suppose, that Hugo had never forgotten young country boys from Arkansas and Georgia who could neither read nor write, bewilderedly drafted into the army and pitted against young Germans who had studied Goethe in the gymnasia—the accumulated masterpieces of literature having apparently not in any way affected the fates of either.

Wilson and Ford understand that memories of the war have more to do with the present than the past.

A most peculiar account of the war is Mary Borden's *The Forbidden Zone*

(1929), which reviewers and readers have always puzzled to adequately describe. Borden was a wealthy Vassar graduate distantly related to both the condenser of milk and the axe-murderer; she was a tomboy, and then a glamorous socialite who funded her own hospital just behind the French lines. It was there, in medical service, that she developed her ambiguous, half-revelatory writing style. Though she had published two books before the war, it was as an independent writer and poet that she lived out the rest of her life.

For her service in the war, Mary Borden was awarded the *Croix de Guerre* and was made a Chevalier of the French Legion of Honor. The whole world had been wrenched by the First World War, and countless lives were distorted in unpredictable ways. A Chicago heiress could not have expected that upon leaving a then demure Vassar she would become a missionary in India, a suffragette, and in two wars would witness horrendous and gruesome assaults on the human body. "There was a man stretched on the table. His brain came off in my hands when I lifted the bandage from his head. It's only one half of his brain." It is not clear if her writing was a way to simply try to bear the savagery and its implications for the twentieth century mind, or if she felt compelled to report scenes in a way that such narrative reports as Sassoon's and Graves' did not do. Like Ford and Wyndham Lewis (the latter an illicit paramour), her subjects and titles convey the ambiguous moral spaces of senses and intellect with which she was concerned. *Sarah Gay* is a story in which a true love affair causes much damage to perfect innocents. Her 1927 novel *Flamingo* (spectral, obscurely referential, oneiric, full of rhymes felt only by the heart), addresses the same scene that Wilson found intriguing in *I Thought of Daisy*: the social dislocations and the literature of New York City in a milieu that found it was forcing itself to question the war's meaning to cultured life. She wrote *Journey down a Blind Alley, Passport for a Girl*, and *Jane—Our Stranger*, each book a broken ambivalence of the heart. Borden was fiercely dedicated to determining the route for her own life, and is properly identified as a feminist. She served several days in jail for throwing a rock through the window of the Chancellor of the Exchequer. When she founded her hospital behind the lines in France, she already had three children.

The Forbidden Zone is poetic and oblique. Its style consists of a strange sort of stoicism, one that reveals the essential heart of sympathetic union by eliminating sentimental attachments; yet the writing retains a Brontesquean intimacy. Her metaphorical writing style has been called visionary, even hallucinatory, as she plumbs to the heart of physical agony, to the process of dying, and to death. Borden wrote of the Apaches who fought in the war: Parisian criminals sentenced to spend the rest of their lives in prison unless they distinguished themselves at the Front, which is to say, killed a substantial number of Germans. In *The Forbidden Zone*, these *enfants malheur* were rendered wholly expendable by both mandarin generals and public sentiment.

In Borden's hospital the very last possible vestige of the glorious enthusiasms that compelled thousands of young British men to join Kitchener's Army is extinguished. *The Forbidden Zone* contemplates the ghastly wartime phenomenon in which—as she describes such an instance in her own hospital—a soldier will commit suicide rather than live with a constant fear of death. Suicide defies the tenets and illusions of what it is to be a human, as it contravenes the perpetuation of the species, aspirations of personal worth, and the possibility of love. Stone crosses and photographs remain, but the only possible living assessment of the war exists in the theatrical narratives played out in our imagination. Quite apart from the difficulty encountered in seeking legitimate reportage that might adequately describe the sorts of things that shrapnel and mortars can do to a body, many writers found no language to convey the nature of the abominations that the war inflicted upon conventional understandings of what it was to be a civilized society. The impossible-to-describe can be very much more easily forgotten, and *pro forma* commemoration allows abandonment: discrete acknowledgments will soon be over.

Virginia Woolf's 1925 novel *Mrs. Dalloway* directs its readers' attention to a matter specific to this war, the effects of shell-shock. Its victims were very often fundamentally unintelligible to the general community.

The novel's interiority and abstracted omniscience mirror the deep privacy that accompanied the consciousness of a soldier lost and alone in the extremity of personal pain and dubious mortality. The mentally wounded soldier Septimus' suicide is set in the context of a frivolous evening party, resembling the city's patrician indifference to the slaughter across the Channel. Woolf was famously prone to dispirit, but is known to have been most especially and morbidly depressed by the hopeless cruelties of the war. Several of her literary works regard the war from within its interior meaning. From the beginning, for Woolf, interpreting the semantics of the whole of the war and its broadest cultural significance was the primary way she learned the war—probably more so than by the newspapers or friends' accounts. The scholar and archivist Karen L. Levenback writes: "[Woolf] saw its experience, on the front or at home, as its history—yet increasingly its constructions had replaced individual memory and become its reality." Thus the final inadequacy of reducing memory of the war to "official language." Levenback continues:

> An important connection among the novels is seen as their narratives focus on the ways characters, or narrators themselves, respond when the language of war is so deprived of its emotional underpinnings that war itself cannot be described.

An acute level of trench authenticity is achieved in John Ellis' *Eye-Deep in Hell* (1976). The title derives from a poem by Ezra Pound, but there is little of the literarily allusive in Ellis' book, which presents an entirely material, infantry soldier's view of the war. Numerous illustrations and drawings depict the sordid fundamentals of the war, not failing to include the latrines, brothels, and propaganda that most books take as granted but rarely portray in full. For other soldiers, nurses are always depicted as maternal in nature, and whores are always venereal. There were episodes of fraternization in the war, and the foe's instances of compassion and forbearance were well known in each army. Incendiary bombs and exploding vantage dirigibles inspired many participants in the war to vivid descriptions of things they had never before known. Soldiers wrote about the earthmud which became their most intimate companion: cold, wet, uncolored, and suggestive of nothing but implacability and misery. All narrative accounts tend to generalize the scenes of the war in an attempt to capture the strange mosaic created by multiple physical effects and the range of emotional sensations, but Ellis more plainly reveals a specificity whose calculation is singular: "In Zonnebeke in 1915 the British and German trenches were only seven or eight yards apart," a proximity easily measured by any reader in his or her living room.

Soldiers spent much of their time marching, or in punitive drills, enforced customarily by centuries-old British habits of deference and obeisance. During stand-to, or in engagement or marching, a soldier was anchored with sixty pounds of equipment; sentries would stand for long hours in the cold and wet. Passchendaele's epical rain, combined with shell holes and cave-ins, added drowning to the myriad fashions of dying. Another brutal asphyxiation was caused by various poisonous gasses, none of which acted rapidly or without excruciation. Across the "millions of deaths" and "pointlessness of the war," Ellis describes the ubiquity of trenchfoot as a constant misery, along with the lice and the millions of rats. A soldier wrote:

> One evening, whilst on patrol, Jacques saw some rats running from under the dead men's greatcoats, enormous rats, fat with human flesh. His heart pounding, he edged towards one of the bodies. Its helmet rolled off. The man displayed a grimacing face, stripped of flesh; the skull bare, the eyes devoured. A set of false teeth slid down on his rotting jacket, and from the yawning mouth leapt an unspeakably foul beast.

The predominant reek was putrefaction. Temporary deafness, from the near-constant explosions turned sound itself into another form of suffocation. Ellis wrote:

> A variety of sounds might be heard in the sudden quiet; the ghostly wail of a shell's screw-cap as it whizzed through the air after an explo-

sion, the plaintive moaning of the men, the buzzing of great swarms
of flies, disturbed by the bombardment, the high-pitched screaming
of the rats, and, sublime absurdity, the singing of the birds.

As a technical matter of battle, impalement by bayonet had queer
visual and aural features, and a sniper's bullet might create but a tickle
in one's throat. Shell splinters caused decapitations by the hundreds
and severed limbs by the thousands. Noses were hacked off, skin was
poached, bodily fluids boiled away; castrations were plentiful. Sleep
deprivation (like dehydration, starvation, and extreme oxygen debt)
formed a field of spectral "otherness," and sensory reductions were
interpreted as a foretaste of death itself. Metaphor is not Ellis' concern.
Physical misery precludes it. There is blood in the mud.

Another medical officer's account of the war, Wilmot Herringham's
1919 *A Physician in France*,[5] insists that it was Prussian militarism alone
that caused the war. It nonetheless confirms Briffault's description of
the scene around Passchendaele as one of unparalleled obliteration and
madness. Herringham reminds us that most of the so-called "wastage"
of lives was due to illness rather than injury: infection, dysentery, suicide, influenza, typhus, meningitis, tetanus. The Boswell scholar Frederick Pottle was an orderly during the war, and writes about his service,
with particular emphasis on war surgery. John McCrae, author of "In
Flanders Field," was also a doctor at an earlier battle at Ypres, where the
death of a close friend led to his composition of the poem most often
associated with the war, sung by school choruses throughout Canada.

Expiring souls in the mud of Passchendaele were far from many things,
but perhaps most especially from the myriad shades of interpretation in
Niall Ferguson's 1998 book *The Pity of War*, a presumptive conclusion
of which is that it was Britain which bore the chief responsibility for the
en garde that led to combat. But if the question of responsibility for the
war did not, as we imagine, occur to the soldiers in the trenches, that
profound riddle was much alive in those who had watched the boys
march off, or among those persons who felt themselves charged with

the duty to explain why debate, economics, and geopolitical matters of empire had somehow leeched into war. A best-seller in England, published in the late fall of 1914, was James M. Beck's virulently polemical *The Evidence in the Case: A Discussion of the Moral Responsibility for the War of 1914, as Disclosed by the Diplomatic Records of England, Germany, Russia, France, Austria, Italy, and Belgium,* the sledge of which falls absolutely upon German political leaders (not the people) as culpable and deserving severe punishment. The omission of any *actual* documentary evidence invalidates Beck's conclusion, and he fails to account for the role of spirit, pride, and greed as possible additional motivators of the armies. Though Beck did not fully realize that the "War of 1914" would evolve into a fifty-month brutal culling of Europe's young men, his citations correctly mention that a large European war was being bruited at least as early as 1911. If the war is not now just memory, but rather a key element of the process by which we turn recollection into the fuel of our own paranoia and the blood of our own lives, one can imagine a eighteen year old boy lying in the mud— as so many did—watching his intestines ooze out of his belly, assessing the logical unlikelihood of rescue, completely unconcerned with theory, and indifferent to recalling whether he was in the German Army or the British Army.

Ernst Junger's *Storm of Steel* was self-published in 1920. He makes clear that there was no such thing as the "German perspective." That conditions were universally horrible has been duly fixed in the historical register, but each chronicler mentions some aspect of the privations no others do: Junger remembers to catalogue, along with the rats and mud and pain and unspeakable boredom and dread, the fact that, additionally, he was menaced with a miserable cold. A friend died, the mortars were inching closer, thirst had become a wracking pain; and on the scene, barely noticed, a snow fell. Erich Maria Remarque was unsurpassed at describing the soldiers' disgust and their quite literal nausea about the stupidity and waste of the war:

> The months pass by. The summer of 1918 is the most bloody and
> the most terrible. The days stand like angels in blue and gold, incom-

prehensible, above the ring of annihilation. Every man here knows that we are losing the war. Not much is said about it, we are falling back, we will not be able to attack again after this big offensive, we have no more men and no more ammunition. Still the campaign goes on – the dying goes on.

The German Army at Passchendaele (2007), by Jack Sheldon, collects diaries and letters from German soldiers at the Front, but it is difficult to detect any inherent Germanness in these accounts, beyond the obvious fact that Germans were facing west and British forces facing east. The propagandists and commanders all portrayed the war as it was required to be seen by vested political forces. At the Battle of Messines, the German Army suffered 22,988 casualties. The event is described by General Sixt von Arnim thus:

> That which was achieved by the German forces of all arms and services, of each unit and formation, through the most obstinate defence and energetic counter-attack and at the cost of severe casualties make this a Day of Honour for us.

It was not only in trench engineering that the German Army benefited from superior organization. Communications were more efficient, including the extensive use of messenger and search dogs. It was a different sense of duty, even if coerced, that allowed the German Army to execute far fewer soldiers for desertion or cowardice, especially compared to the French, for whom mutinies and refusals were for a time commonplace. And there was something in the German vernacular that allowed, if not exactly dissent, at least the sort of alternate opinion that was more efficiently tamped down in Britain. Crown Prince Rupprecht of Bavaria noted in August of 1917 that General Ludendorff "stated that if we were to vacate Belgium we could have peace." All soldiers knew this. They hated the conditions and the ugliness, and yet, soldiers in both armies when pressed to action, displayed stunning and bold acts of courage. Adolph Hitler was a runner and cyclist at Passchendaele (and much despised by his *kamaraden* for his grubby war-enthusiasm), but in both armies runners and guides generally were especially admired. A German officer wrote:

> Heavy shell fire rained down on Passchendaele. Fire was coming down all around a large crucifix—Christ covered in filth—which stood in the middle of the main street. All the telephone lines were cut. Then the runners had to take over. Runners! What responsibility to duty, what silent, sacrificial, gallantry that word covers!

Briffault loathed the eager totalitarian nature that would later degenerate into fascism, and his letters from Zillebeke and Passchendaele plainly cite the damage Boche forces inflict, but he cannot have much differentiated the final effects that national and class politics would have on the human body in his care, maimed and extinguished.

The slaughter continued apace, yet two soldiers were alone in a shell hole. The wounded man tended to the dying man with grace and affection. Together they were "daydreaming," Vizefeldwebel Alfred Kleysteuber remarked, as the Berliner cradled the expiring Cardiff Fusilier.

Finally, as the Battle of Third Ypres Passchendaele turned nominally toward a British "victory," interrogation officer Oberleutnant Muller-Albert reported in his findings the belief held by his British prisoners that "Only the newspapers in England and those who are profiting from the war wish it to continue." But in Germany, as the home populations wearied of starvation and deprivation, Offizierstellvertreter von Gelshorn wrote. "A lot of what has been going on in Germany is shameful for our Fatherland. All the blood would have flowed in vain." As it had indeed been a war for markets and honor, and not a war of conquest and occupation, a German victory might not have changed the life of the Paris dance halls very much at all. Some scholars have suggested that a German victory could hardly have been worse than the actual damage done over fifty-two months of slaughter and desecration.

Denis Winter's 1985 book *Death's Men—Soldiers of the Great War* is a lyrical abstraction, in contrast to the more plain-spoken trench accounts.

Some of the stories are familiar, and the activities of the soldiers are not particularly distinguishable from many other accounts, but Winter's voice describes the soldiers' thoughts with an emphasis on their social being, as creatures of cultural institutions and specific societal groups. The soldiers' interior lives float amid their individual senses of aesthetics, their indignities, their dreams and primitive psychology; their cosmology. We might recalibrate our understanding of the limits of human endurance, for evidence is plentiful that extremes were exceeded, especially in regards to enduring horrifying and atrocious scenes. Winter's touch with words as he describes the men, and his nuanced regard for a soldier's privacies of heart and mind, display much elegance and love. It is no surprise that, in these contexts, events we might have called supernatural come to us as straightforward information about warfield events. These include spectral visitations and premonitions (Wiesel's *Souls on Fire* comes to mind), examples of man's unimaginable adaptability to bedlam, and acts of instantaneous generosity. Many participant-chroniclers of the war recalled scenes of sheer beauty at the front: in mucky and desecrated Belgium and eastern France there were sunrises seen through sulfurous clouds of phosgene gas that made rainbows. Blunden referred to a "sunset all seraphim and cherubim." Starscapes seen through the explosions' vibrations diffused light itself; and a beatific look on the face of an expiring friend elevated empathy from despair to the sublime. Thus they too saw formed before them elements of life that only novelists and philosophers had previously been able to bring into view: "fellowship," and "brotherhood," and "pity," and even the pre-Existentialist vacancy of Kierkegaard's "*existents-forhold.*" Men expected death, and had been much immersed in its scenes; they had surely held countless conversations about the details of the different manners of expiration and decease. If a matter of quiet acceptance appeared for some men to be embracing the subject of the exercise (they were replaceable war-machines hurled onto peril and then discarded), they might also have experienced episodes of clairvoyance or time-travel. Last-minute epiphanies may have revealed the dark and infinite nothing, though such metaphysical characterizations are the province mostly for the far-away and long ago, and "everything is a metaphor" was not a particularly useful consideration for those expiring at the bottom of a foul trench. They might years later employ the term Technicolor or 3-D to begin to describe the bizarre images and concussive sounds at the zenith of a battle, and an inadequate term for this interconnectedness might be synaesthesia, yet that will perhaps begin to suggest the weird consonance of unlikes that mesmerized and afflicted soldiers exposed to such disarray.

George L. Mosse, in *Fallen Soldiers* (1990) examines the cult of commemoration for the men sacrificed to nationalism's most brutal excess. It is a beautiful and quite lyrical contemplation of mortality and memory, the deeply mythical aspects of the cooperative will of the German people, and the more chilly reserve of Britain's mourning, particularly as seen in cemeterial design. For many soldiers entrance into the armies provided an escape from various paternalistic tyrannies, and fraternal obeisance seemed balmy by comparison. The romantic German Youth Movement impelled young men to the near-knighthood promised by joining the brotherhood of the Army: "Strength was equated with restfulness, as opposed to the love of chaos. Here the past was alive, in the stories told by the Youth Movement, in their medieval dances and plays, while expressionists and futurists, by contrast, rejected the past and thought history a burden imposed upon youth." In this respect Mosse is indebted to Walter Flex's 1916 book *Wanderer zwischen beiden Welten*, (*The Wanderer between Two Worlds*). Youth devoted to *wandervogel* slipped faultlessly into the German army, and into the nation's reframing of the justification and subsequent continuance of the First World War. Flex was killed in 1917 in Estonia: his epitaph reads: "He who swears on Prussia's flag has nothing left that belongs to himself."

Such cultural tides as the *wandervogel* imperceptibly directed the thoughts of young men and fattened their wills for adventure, the resolution of which was invisible and mattered little. They had already been striving to differentiate themselves from their fathers; they were eager for travel, and hoped to add to their *palmarès* and thereby attract women or improve their chances at rising in the social echelons. Farmers and city workers were fervent to burst out of lives that promised to be dull. German youth had been steeped in the florid sentiments centered around the *Sturm und Drang*, and preconditioned by the immensely persuasive such books as Goethe's *The Sorrows of Young Werther*. The notion of death was associated with heroic beliefs and definitive acts. Richard Wagner's operas exalted a valorous nature that was taken to be inherent in German culture. These artworks' titanic characters and intrepid chivalries derived from ancient Germanic archetypes. *Parsifal*'s grail knights, and *Der Ring des Niebelungen*'s many fantasizing strivers formed the noble mythology of Germany's impressionable youth. (Perceval may be Arabic in origin: *fal parsi*: pure fool.) In England, Arthurial legend did not constitute itself so practically; rather, the English cast of mind referred to imperialist notions of its role in shepherding the world with its elevated morals and graces. The extent of these sources' direct influence on those who go off to war is questionable, but can lead to telling conjectures: Canadian boys may have detected the opportunity to express national yearnings; Australian roustabouts could show delicate London shop boys how wars really are fought. American enthusiasm was perhaps an overflow of continental western expansion. Sikhs were predisposed to martial dominance and martyrism: they were known as the Black Lions. Freud's conceptions of the tension between collective war and individual freedom were formed in large part by his study of the First World War. In his 1930 book *Civilization and its Discontents*, Freud understood war and its slaughter as instinctual aggression, death drive, libidinal release, an acceptable locale for sadism and masochism, a false religion, and deep-rooted hunger for power. For Werther, sex and death were the same. His suicide was the only possible fruition.

But no national generalization can be sustained when culled in equal measure are dreamers and farmers and men and women expecting to sit with a deity a second after the cessation of their earthly life. Death was, there, divorced absolutely from notions of the nation-state or economics, and men saw that the transition was a personal matter, in the way that they had previously understood their own autobiography.

Because of the distortions of consciousness, our own times might say that soldiers were "unstuck in time" (Vonnegut), and that they experienced ur-Jungian detections and recognitions, interlacing of undifferentiated symbols and signifiers, and even Warholian uncoverings of the supernatural reciprocation between the banal and the sublime. Gaudier-Brzeska wrote from the trenches to Dorothy Shakespear that the constant bombardments and explosions prevented his men from dreaming adequately, anticipating the science of REM sleep, found to be crucial to a person's emotional stability and sense of well-being. There were many Portuguese soldiers at Passchendaele; Scots and outback men; Maoris, Fijians, Senegalese, Newfoundlanders, Afrikaans, Sikhs, and Chinese and African labor gangs; genetic codes were mingling in the mad material distortion. Did those streams of hereditary signifiers teleport? Was mind-reading really possible? Were memories only one's own? We read of delusional psychosis and living ghosts, temporary aphasia, and schizophrenia. In such extreme conditions of despair and tribulation, there was a range of unique possibilities for experiencing one's own humanity. The theatre of war presented to the soldier heinous scenes of dismemberment and ooze, "a face detached from its skull." The scenes stretched their understanding of what they believed could occur, but it was a disbelief from which there was no suspension. Their growing accustomed to such barbarities was less an earned stoicism than it was a complete reorientation of their paradigmatic moral pinions. Many soldiers remarked the never-before-seen visage of their fellows, waiting in the trench for the whistles that will halve their number and maim many more; eyes saw "beyond," in glows of spectral evocation. In such extremities of the admixture of a personal future and terminal mortality, may we not also imagine that visions were urgently and truly realized? The brain's electro-chemical circuitries spark occurrences we might call otherworldly or parapsychological: life flashing before their eyes, impossible associative connections flaring; they heard voices; they observed themselves from above. Do these distortions extend to episodes of telepathy, prescience, infantile memories, and clairvoyance? Amid the illusory, fantastical, and metaphysical manifestations in the trenches, the soldiers knew well the incongruity that Samuel Beckett expressed in his plays, when marching they sang together, to the tune, of all things, "Auld Lang Syne":

> We're here because we're here because we're here because we're here
> We're here because we're here because we're here because we're here

All accounts of the war mention the impending stroke of inevitable resolution that was assured by the arrival of American troops and their inexhaustible material resources. These would, in fact, have proved conclusive, and England's forces were trying to hold out until their arrival. The German forces sought to devise a last gust of strategy that might prevent the certain loss of the war due to the Yankee oil, steel, and regiments of supremely fit "gangsters." The Americans' arrival also revealed another fact about the last year of the war, during which the Germans who were captured and killed were remarked to be tired old men or callow boys, almost all of them underfed and sickly. The war finally turned on German impoverishment of resources and food. Vera Brittain was dispirited by the appearance of the British soldiers; they too were pitiably decrepit or weakened. When a troop of American soldiers marches by, late in the war, she is awe-struck by their robust beauty and their gleaming health.

In America ragtime and its implicit carnality was maturing into jazz and its overt sexuality; American boys occupied the estaminets with a new flavor of vigor. Though it is perhaps too simple a judgment, in Germany there was no equivalent of carnal dance, and it took the sanguine theatre of Brecht and Weill, and the Weimar Republic, to allow the German people to discover that carnal rhythms also pulsed through their bodies. Following the war: the licentious 1920s.

Philip Gibbs was a freelance correspondent whose wartime reports, to contemporary sensibilities, read much like the other journalism of the day, in that they are both chauvinistic and bowdlerized. Censors prohibited mention of locations, strategic reverses, or numbers of men killed. Yet the book he published in 1920 is titled *Now It Can Be Told*, and is a straightforward description of the wrongs of strategy perpetrated upon populations of British and Commonwealth innocents. As has been noted, soldiers' writings about the war were routinely concise and unexpectedly expressive, often eloquent. Gibbs was not a proponent of the modern literary idiom—social and personal. His descriptions are deftly flavored with environmental context, not excluding the sort of detail that might import our own senses into the scene. Walking through a strafe of artillery and shrapnel, "I noticed how loudly and sweetly the larks were singing up in the blue. Several horses lay dead, newly killed, with blood oozing about them, and their entrails smoking." Gibbs had in 1915 published *The Soul of War*, a book that may be the first to assess the existential dread and acedia that affronted the soldiers in the trenches, and which is cited as an early seed of the impassivity and disaffection that would after the war become the sensibility of "the lost generation."

In *The Middle Parts of Fortune*, Frederick Manning presents a trench view of the war, and like all other accounts by the British, a basic sort of veiling and bookish English prose softens the reality of the conditions and the depth of the dejection. The book was originally published in 1930, with an equally poetic, but perhaps more realistic title, *Her Privates We* (Guildenstern addressing Hamlet). The book is said to have had a great effect on Hemingway, who claimed that he read it once a year to recall what the war was really like.

In a book that *Le Libertaire* called "the most beautiful book ever written on the tragic events that blood-stained Europe," Gabriel Chevallier's *La Peur* (*Fear*) recounts the autobiographical story of his time as an infantryman in the French Army. He was awarded the Croix de Guerre and the Chevalier de la Légion d'honneur, though Chevallier emphasizes the misery of the trench and the ways he had devised to elude particularly dangerous missions. He served from 1915 through to the end of the war, enduring its privations and disgusts, and the French Army's mutinies and tactical blunders.

> Men are foolish and ignorant. Hence their misery. Instead of think-ing, they believe what they are told, what they are taught. They choose leaders and masters without judging them, with a fatal taste for slavery. Men are sheep. Which is why armies and wars are possi-ble. They die victims of their stupid docility.

Chevallier was wounded and for a long while hospitalized. A nurse asked him what he did at the front. He responded: "I was afraid."

Leon Wolff's 1958 history *In Flanders Field: The 1917 Campaign* is among the first analyses to overtly question Sir Douglas Haig's competence to conduct the strategies and tactics at Passchendaele. Haig was, from the beginning, temperamentally unsuited to a war of attrition, with which he had no experience. The concept of the usefulness of the air forces came to him slowly, and tanks had never figured in the war he knew, of cavalry and positional movement. He chose exactly the wrong person to be the final arbiter of supplying him with information, Brigadier General John Charteris, who was a noted propagandist and non-analytical administrator, and who had never been trained in military intelligence. Wolff separates himself from the historical narrative, providing us with what has become an almost clinical view of the conditions and forms of the war.

Contemplating the war's immense necrology and vast moral damage, it is possible to forget that various technicians view the war and its bat-tles with minds trained on a specific system within it: hydrologists see simple solutions to the flooding, and nutritionists wonder at the valueless fare. Military historians and tacticians examine the debacle of Passchendaele with item-level particulars and deconstructive analysis, the sort of exegesis to which expressions of pathos regarding the dead can unfortunately seem only incidentally attached. Robin Pryor and Trevor Wilson's *Passchendaele: The Untold Story* seeks to establish a neutral view of the opposing forces' activities. Philip Warner's history *Passchendaele,* published by Pen & Sword Military Classics Ltd. in 2005, has perhaps the widest scope of discussing political and military strategies and tactics, the attempts by soldiers to explain the battles, and the culpability of General Haig's lethal obstinacy.

When the village of Passchendaele was finally won (by Canadian forces and their superior training, resources, and heart), an English general could look over the accomplishment with some pride in his boys, but he would also have seen on the horizon nothing but charred tree stands, and heaps of smoking bricks. Ashes and Dust. After Pass-chendaele, General Kiggell visited the front lines for the first time, and, surveying the mud and the uncountable bodies lost and dead in the mud, gasped "My God! Did we really send our men to fight in *this?*" The land was handed back to the German forces in April of 1918. Today it is green and beautiful, a flowering farmland. One day it will be seafloor.

There is general appreciation for and admiration of Paul Fussell's signal accomplishment *The Great War and Modern Memory.* Since an alternate premise may be that it is not memory, specifically, that keeps the war within us, but our living out its moral lesson, this may be viewed as a contradiction of Fussell's gift. No one alive today fought at Passchendaele. All memories are derived. We may have once seen a movie or half-recalled a book. We therefore require specificities: we must have corpulent rats between our knees, and a thousand lice chewing our skin. Thousands of books by participants and scholars have been written about the war. Internet sources abound,[6] with freshly discovered and published memoirs, images, and interpretations. All of these have their readers, but that is now a matter of being specially interested in the subject. As part of the vast public consciousness, the war has slipped into the unspecific fog of the past. In 2014, in the New York Barnes and Noble "Military History" shelves, there are three hundred titles. Five are about World War I. Modern memory philosophizes about and sentimen-talizes the First World War in a way that can only ever be entirely ratless.

Adam Hochschild alone has written of the peace movement in Europe, in *To End All Wars* (2011). The voice of the appeal for peace in England and Germany was sometimes vivid, but was more often altogether ignored by the very families who sent soldiers and officers to the European massacre. The Pacifists' voice was amplified (and simultaneously diluted) by the moral movements of women's emancipation, Irish Home Rule, and variant forms of socialism. The peace protest existed mostly in the minds of persons able to afford themselves the luxury of a philosophic view. Stopping the slaughter may have been an ultimate goal, but the cause was carried out chiefly by declamation and the written word, forces quite useless against explosive bombs and piercing bayonets. If the war was a political game, so was its counterforce, but no political movement could approach the effects of combat; it was always, first, slaughter. Margaret Hobhouse reported in Sylvia Pankhurst's publication *Women's Dreadnought* that "the German occupation was nowhere near as cruel as the British burning of Boer farms in South Africa," but Hochschild reports that "the Germans had been brutal; in addition to deliberately shooting more than 5,000 Belgian civilians and setting fire to thousands of buildings, they had poured gasoline into the famous university library at Louvain and burned it to the ground, along with its priceless collection of 230,000 books and 750 medieval manuscripts." Objection to the war took the form of voluntary imprisonments and hunger strikes, news of which gestures rarely reached the boys in the trenches. Natural moments of concord did occur, as with the Christmas Peace of 1914, when opposing soldiers met in No Man's Land for fraternal greetings and football, and there were an uncountable number of acts of brotherhood between wounded foes on the battlefield, though no meaningful rapprochement was generalized by these spontaneous fellowships. Social animals made the war, but neither the pacifist movement nor grand political governments could stop it. It was only degeneration and exhaustion that wrought an end to engaged warfare, though the sentiments pertaining to markets and paranoia would prevail for years.

The esteemed historian Lyn McDonald's aggregation of soldiers' voices—from letters home, diaries, interviews, and obituary reports—most clearly delineates the difference between that which is spoken by its participants, and the language used by professional writers to convey the war, the latter sometimes deformed almost to Tennysonian lyric. In her book *They Called It Passchendaele*, we are reminded that the German Army constantly endured an additional trauma and trial, that of near-starvation. And in late March of 1918, skirmishes resulted in blood seeping into the ground at the exact spot where blood had seeped into the ground upon the broken battlefields of the 1916 Battle of the Somme. The soldiers described their experiences with wonder, and they usually acknowledged that they could never do a really satisfactory job of illustrating the carnage. Though these letters home had great currency, they often wanted to spare the home folk the true details; moreover, when they touched the shores of home again, many wanted nothing more than to forget what they had seen and felt. In any case, they soon became occupied with trying to find a job, or a place to live, or a way to hide their missing eye, or hand, or leg, or arm, or face.

A contemporary description of the years immediately preceding and following the Great War is expressed in Juliet Nicolson's 2006 *The Perfect Summer* and 2009's *The Great Silence*. The war was a monstrous blot on Europe, a pivot from which there was neither recovery nor relief from the unspoken truth that everyone knew: the war was pointless. Nicolson's grandfather was present at Versailles, affording her the chance to hear about the feeling in the room that had been inadequately described by the newspapers. Winston Groom's 2002 *A Storm in Flanders* offers perhaps the most concise explanation of the causes leading to war. The book also pays especially close attention to the topography.

Paul Gross' 2008 movie and book *Passchendaele* reveal the breadth and blood of his keen sympathy (his grandfather fought at Passchendaele), though the story is styled with a love story and Canadiana. Similarly, despite creditable recreations of the scene, the 2012 film *Beneath Hill 60* squeezes the consequences of the 1914-1918 War into the social and psychological patterns of 2014. The result is not only an offense against soldiers' individual sacrifices but it assures that we will remember the war in an only contemporaneous way. Our empathy would be strengthened rather, by examining our own world through the eyes of those in the trenches.

Another, crucial visual depiction of the war comes from the Australian photographer Frank Hurley, who was marooned with Shackleton in Antarctica until August of 1916, and thereafter shipped to Europe, where he created essential images of Passchendaele. Some of the photographs' documentary authenticity may have been compromised by overlay, but none diminished (or could ever equal) the horror of the killing grounds there. Similarly, a fair number of journalists' films of the war were newsreel recreations, but neither do these conceal the wasted topography of denuded trees and shell-pocked earth, and the evident lack of fitness in the soldiers.

Other media convey the war, including art and sculpture. The American Claggett Wilson's paintings seem to emphasize the explosions and fire, but dark in the corners of his canvas are grotesque Kafkaesque figures, reminding us of the sublimated pathology of the martial show. The German artist George Grosz was excused for medical reasons from the German Army, and his outrage at the atrocities of war took the form of his famous painting *The Funeral*. Painted in 1917 and 1918, it is a futurist and cubist display of human grotesqueries. Grosz describes this artwork:

> In a strange street by night, a hellish procession of dehumanized figures mills, their faces reflecting alcohol, syphilis, plague ... I painted this protest against a humanity that had gone insane. I had grown up in a humanist atmosphere, and war to me was never anything but horror, mutilation and senseless destruction, and I knew that many great and wise people felt the same way about it . . . I thought the war would never end. And perhaps it never did, either.

Other artists were pulled into the war by the chance patrimony of their nation-states. Fritz Kreisler's *Four Weeks in the Trenches–The War Story of a*

Violinist, describes the entirety of his service, during which his peculiar gifts of hearing served the technicians of the mortar corps:

> at the Front, the extreme uncertainty of the morrow tended to lessen the interest in the details of today; consequently I may have missed a great many interesting happenings alongside of me which I would have wanted to note under other circumstances. One gets into a strange, psychological, almost hypnotic state of mind on the firing line which probably prevents the mind's eye from observing things in a normal way.

We may think of Rainer Maria Rilke, the fragile child of Bohemia, providing such service to the Austrian army as he could—drawing lines on the paper to be used in the calculations for artillery. He cannot have been the only tenderly sensitive man taken into an army that had no use for such fragile weeds, but no written history recalls the persons who simply withered or were crushed out of existence by service in the armed forces even before the atrocities at the front.

Artists' work was doubtless transformed by their acquaintance with death, acedia, unreality, and living in the most extreme state of life's conditionality, and persons in other vocations had the horrors splined into their memories. The French artist Fernand Léger was injured at Verdun; he wrote of "the crudeness, variety, humour and downright perfection of certain men around me." Auguste Macke was killed in the second month of the war, having already established himself at the vanguard of the expressionists who were practically inventing the use of extreme color. His later work was muted somewhat, by the coming of the war. Did Georges Braque's abstract cubism foresee the strange disruptions and physical rearrangements of form on the western front? The architect Walter Gropius was severely wounded in the war; in 1919 he founded the Bauhaus movement in architecture and design, which rejected ornamentation and moved from expressionism to the New Objectivity. Bureaucrats formed their realpolitik conceptions in the war: the OSS was directed by William "Wild Bill" Donovan, who served with Joyce Kilmer in the Fighting 69th; Donovan's highly decorated service in 1918 doubtless colored his career as the father of the CIA. The British soldier George Catlin fought in Belgium at the end of the war. Subsequently he would become a prominent proponent of the new discipline of political science, and after the war he would meet and marry Vera Brittain. Conscientious objectors, Americans, and artists whose temperaments or gender prevented their frontline service drove ambulances or transport vehicles: Edmund Wilson, Archibald MacLeish, John Dos Passos, E.M. Forster, baseball executive Warren Giles, Jean Cocteau, Somerset Maugham, Ernest Hemingway, Lester Pearson, Dashiell Hammett, James M. Cain, e. e. cummings, Malcolm Cowley, William Wellman (who directed the 1927 Oscar-winning film *Wings*, based in part on his time first as an ambulance driver, then as a flyer—he was nicknamed "Wild Bill" and awarded the Croix de Guerre); Harry Crosby (whose eventual suicide might be understood in the specific terms of Baudelaire and Poe), and Gertrude Stein ("Let me recite what history teaches. History teaches."). Harvard, Yale, Princeton, and Cornell contributed a large proportion of the young men and women to the Lafayette Escadrille and to the Norton-Harjes Ambulance Corps. Most of these students were persons of commitment and brio, but the Escadrille also attracted the inveterate scoundrel and crook Bert Hall, a Missouri ne'er-do-well and shirker who was dismissed from the Corps. The champion Olympic fencer Nedo Nadi served in the Royal Italian Army, winning gold medals before and after the war. Kansan Robert McAlmon served with the American Air Corps, and proceeded immediately following the war to become one of the very earliest publishers of Pound, Wallace Stevens, and William Carlos Williams, and he had the honor of typing and editing his friend Joyce's manuscript of *Ulysses*. A French guide of Hoggson's American Industry Commission was Henri-Pierre Roché, author of the novel *Jules et Jim*, in which the war provides the apposite context for the doomed lovers. These ancillary aides still encountered wounded men with unstanchable flows, severed arms, legs, and heads.

Writers disposed to paradigms and abstractions will have seen much to fulfill a literature of dread. Raymond Chandler fought with the Royal Highlanders in the French trenches, the *noir* unfolding before him, enwrapping him in the strange permanence of evil. The hard-boiled detective genre: who could be more tough and realistic (shall we say, who is more literal, and unillusioned?) than a soldier freezing and hungry in the mud contemplating his own death? Louis-Ferdinand Céline was wounded at the first battle of Ypres in 1915: his most famous novel is the nihilistic *Journey to the End of the Night*. The painter Albert (Rothenstein) Rutherston served in Palestine, and wrote Dora Carrington: "I'm firmly convinced that in the end the war will be a good thing." He hoped that war might cure art of "the unreal and the trivial." Paul Nash was one of several painters who suffered injury as an infantryman and transferred to the English government's War Propaganda Bureau; Nash created necessarily dark canvases of the war scenes, one of which is entitled *We Are Making a New World*. William Orpen was another official war artist; in addition to formal ceremonial portraits of politicians paying site-visits safely away from the front, he painted harrowing images of dead bodies at Zonnebeke, among the grimmest pictorial representations to come out of the war. Unlike other war artists who managed to shake the horror from their minds, Orpen was depressed, and lived until 1931 morally dismayed by what he had seen and depicted. German artist Otto Dix fought at the Somme and on the Eastern Front, and participated in the doomed Spring Offensive, Germany's last thrust and hope, which exposed the pathetic state of the country's forces and its collapsed morale. Many of Dix's expressionist and dadaesque works reference the war which had traumatized him, and he published *Der Krieg*, a collection of etchings, in 1924. The sculptor Henry Moore served with the Prince of Wales' Own Civil Service Rifles; at the Battle of Cambrai he was incapacitated by a gas attack. Writers Charles Nordhoff and James Norman Hall of the *Bounty* trilogy both served with the Lafayette Escadrille. Hall was shot down and languished in a German prisoner-of-war camp until the Armistice. The painter, sculptor, and poet Max Ernst served as an artillery officer, who regarded his service in the German Army as quite literally the period of his death followed by his resurrection. His friend and close collaborator Hans Arp eluded service in the army by emigrating to neutral Switzerland. Franz Kafka tried to enlist, but was rejected on medical grounds. R.C. Sherriff was severely wounded at Passchendaele; in later life he wrote the screenplay for *Goodbye Mr. Chips*. Novelist Simon Evans fought with the Cheshires, and was badly injured by gas. Evans died at age forty-four of respiratory disease, one soldier of many who carried the war's damages to an early death. English composer Ralph Vaughan Williams served originally as a stretcher-bearer, but then shifted to combat duty in the trenches. His hearing was injured by the shell fire, and later in life he became completely deaf. The British monument sculptor Charles Jagger was repeatedly wounded at Gallipoli and on the western front; these injuries were directly responsible for his death in 1934. The composer Alban Berg served for four years in the Austro-Hungarian Army, during and after which he composed his opera *Wozzeck*, an atonal expression of abstract musical forms and a brutalist depiction of privation that calls to mind the dislocations and disharmonies he had experienced during the war. Max Beckmann served as a medical orderly; were his post-war expressionist paintings a result of his shell-shock? Was his *Neue Sachlichkeit* a result of an excess of subjective, emotional interiority during his traumatic war? Expressionism flowered immediately after the war, the visual and theatrical arts adumbrating the ensuing protests against conventional practice.

The German playwright and dramaturg Frank Wedekind had, before the war, seemed to anticipate both stage expressionism and epic theatre, with its dissociative melanges and seemingly pointless utterances. Wedekind died in Munich in March of 1918, of causes unrelated to the war. Wedekind wrote that the only sin was the sin against the flesh: "Nature was contrasted with ossified custom, the decayed order of the word. Dead custom has deromanticized everything, so that Mephistopheles is nothing but an insurance agent." A fair description of the Great War.

The composer Maurice Ravel served as a truck driver at Verdun and elsewhere during the war; this was doubtless a traumatizing assignment for a sensitive person of ill health, but it was during his war service that he composed *le tombeau de Couperin*, each movement of which is dedicated to a friend who had been killed in the war. Despite the rampant nationalism occasioned by the war, he refused to join the National League for the Defense of French Music, writing that "it would be dangerous for French composers to ignore systematically the works of their foreign colleagues, and thus form themselves into a sort of national coterie: our musical art, so rich at the present time, would soon degenerate and become isolated by its own academic formulas." Like some few other common soldiers and accidental philosophers, Ravel hadn't possessed the sufficient self-deception that convinced different flagbearers to kill a farmer like themselves, a fisherman like themselves, or a violinist like themselves.

Though his actual war service was limited to being an orderly in a venereal disease hospital, there was more of the war in Bertholt Brecht's Berlin dramas than ever appeared afterward on the London stage. So, his epic theatre: *The Threepenny Opera's* antiheroic Macheath, and the No Man's Land desolation in *Rise and Fall of the City of Mahagonny*: can these be fully imagined without the war? His Marxism? (And from Brecht may we find derived Godard, Fassbender, and Pina Bausch?) Other expressionists had served in the war: Kokoschka, Klee, and Egon Schiele, the last of whom died of Spanish flu in October of 1918. Ludwig Wittgenstein volunteered in the Austro-Hungarian army, serving heroically; he spent nine months in an Italian prisoner-of-war camp. His brother Paul, a classical pianist, fought in the army, was shot, and had his right arm amputated. His brother Kurt was an officer in the Austrian army; he committed suicide in October of 1918 when the troops under his command deserted. Gabriele d'Annunzio was a paramount warmonger and Italian nationalist; some of his pronouncements encouraged Mussolini's fascism. Mussolini served as a soldier, and was wounded by an exploded mortar. G.K. Chesterton's brother Cecil died weeks after the Armistice of a disease contracted in the trenches; he was a socialist turned Distributist, a right-wing Catholic, anti-Semite, and vigorous enthusiast of the war. The British playwright J.B. Priestley served with the Duke of Wellington's regiment; his autobiography *Margin Released* bitterly pillories the British officer class that condemned so many lower-class soldiers to their death. The art historian, curator, and poet Laurence Binyon, aged forty-five, served as a hospital orderly and stretcher bearer; he was a central figure in the Modernist movement that attended to Asian influences in art and literature. The long and strange career of the French modernist writer Blaise Cendrars does not directly reference his service in the French Foreign Legion at the Somme where he lost an arm, though his main works are *La Main coupée* and *J'ai tué*. Like Briffault, he passed the Second World War with difficulty, in Paris. British soldiers C.S. Lewis, J.R.R. Tolkien, Hugh Lofting, and A.A. Milne wrought Narnia, hobbits, Doolittle, and Pooh; work they fashioned in the Great War became our standard escapist literature. If our sympathetic empathy aligns with certain literary sensibilities, perhaps no soldier-author provides a more conclusive transport into the trenches of war than Herbert Read. Read served with distinction in France. His first books of poetry, *Songs of Chaos*, and *Naked Warriors*, were imagist and metaphysical in nature, and derived from his experiences under fire. His literary career was concerned with the philosophy of good writing (*English Prose Style*); as an art critic he championed surrealism and noted the influence of existentialism. A proponent of Freud, and then Jung, Read identified himself as an anarchist. His brother Charles was killed in 1918. One of his most harrowing war poems is about a deserter: "The Execution of Cornelius Vane."

Henri Gaudier-Brzeska (the *Savage Messiah*) was killed at Neuville St. Vaast in 1915. A friend of Ezra Pound, Wyndham Lewis, and Jacob Epstein, his sculpture is now associated with the blunt visions of the war, though almost all his work actually preceded the violence: vectored planes, vaguely-representational impressions, and force are the objective correlatives of what he observed in European culture before the war. Pound's erudition and irascibility are evident in 1916's *A Memoir of Gaudier-Brzeska*, one of the only direct treatments of the intersection of art and such matters as war, if war can be thought of as an extension of the more invidious and ugly aspects of human nature. Vorticism derived from persons who had been previously interested in imagism, and each was an appropriate way of trying to replicate and explain the appearance of the battlefields. Pound's book about Gaudier-Brzeska can have been written by no one but himself, with its numerous languages, juxtapositions, and sudden shifts of tone, subject, and sympathies. The book, like his "Cantos," and like the war itself, resists being paraphrased or explained by conventional discourse. We may wonder what Gaudier-Brzeska might have achieved in later life, just as we measure the countless lost later lives of every man and woman killed in the war. But the sculptor need not be limited to speculations on what might have been, though his relative obscurity seems in part fueled by our surmise of the never-realized work. Gaudier was a visionary, and in his practical life, derived his choices and actions from such visions; he assumed the surname of his rather older and mentally unstable Polish mistress, Sophie Brzeska. His thinking was always sculptural, and his letters from the trenches easily mix reporting on the conditions of the war and his keen interest in the artistic and intellectual life in Paris and London. Writing from the Front:

> Our woods are magnificent. I am just now quartered in trenches in the middle of them, covered with lily of the valley, it grows and flowers on the trench itself. In the night we have many nightingales to keep us company. They sing very finely and the loud noise of the attacks and counter-attacks does not disturb them in the least. It is very warm and nice out of doors, one does not mind sleeping out on the ground now.
>
> Yes I have survived and will continue to do so, I am absolutely sure. We are at rest to-day after a week's trench life. We have had rain, mud, sunshine, bullets, shells, shrapnels, sardines, and fun. I am ordered for night patrol. We are only four in the company for this work. We set out at sun-down and come back at dawn. This time we must go to explore an old bombarded mill within the German line where a maxim-gun is in position. We shall have luck I have a good presentiment. . . . I started with two men to reinforce wire entangle-

ments at a few yards off the enemy. We were undisturbed for a long time, my fellows went on driving poles and I was busy setting wires lying on my back when the silly moon shone out of the mist. The Germans caught sight of me and then pumpumpumpumpumpum-pumpum their bullets cut four barbed wires just above my face and I was in a funny way indeed caught by the loose wire. I grasped my rifle at last and let them have the change, but it was a signal: my men lost their heads, one let his rifle fall into his wire coil, threw away the wooden mallet and jumped into the trench as a wild rabbit, the other in his wake, but the latter did not forget the gun. When they came in they said I was dead, and to avenge me my lieutenant ordered volley firing, the boches did the same, and I got between the two. At great risk I came back to the trench, where my lieutenant was very aston-ished. When the row ceased and the fog set in again I went back with my two chaps, found everything back and completed the wire snares. I got your letter and replied. I am beginning the essay [on Vorticism] now. . . . Anyway, no one foresaw the awful ground we had to defend. We must keep two bridges and naturally as usual 'until death.' We cannot come back to villages to sleep, and we have to dig holes in the ground which we fill with straw and build a roof over, but the soil is so nasty that we find water at two feet six inches depth; and even if we stop at a foot, which is hardly sufficient to afford cover, we wake up in the night through the water filtering up the straw. The beastly regiment which was here before us remained three months, and as they were all dirty miners used to all kinds of dampness they never did an effort to better the place up a bit. When we took the trenches after the march it was a sight worthy of Dante, there was at the bot-tom a foot deep of liquid mud in which we had to stand two days and two nights, rest we had in small holes nearly as muddy, add to this a position making a V point into the enemy who shell us from three sides, the close vicinity of 800 putrefying German corpses, and you are at the front in the marshes of the Aisne. . . . the foremost trench element near Neuville St. Vaast, a continual bombardment and end-less inferno. I have been buried twice in the trench, have had a shell bursting in the middle of a dozen grenades, which miraculously did not explode, and men nastily wounded to whom I must give first aid. We are betting on our chances, whose turn it is next. The boches are restless but we pay them well, they dared attack the day before yesterday. It has been a lurid death dance. . . . To-day is magnificent, a fresh wind, clear sun and larks singing cheerfully. The shells do not disturb the songsters. In the Champagne woods the nightingales took no notice of the fight either. They solemnly proclaim man's foolery and sacrilege of nature. I respect their disdain.

Seven days later, he was killed.

In Jean Renoir's film *Grand Illusion*, it is a simple matter to forget which side you are on. In Clifford Odets 1944 film *None but the Lonely Heart*, the father of Ernie Mott, the main character, was killed in the war. Ernie is sometimes called by another name, "Verdun," instead of his own. Persons we might never associate with the Great War were participants in the broad stage of death: the astronomer Edwin Hubble, Walter Brennan, Angelo Roncalli (Pope John XXIII). Alan Seeger, an uncle of Pete Seeger and a Harvard classmate of T.S. Eliot, was killed at the Battle of the Somme. The infamous New York City gangster Monk Eastman served in the Army with distinction at the age of forty three, returned to America, immediately reverted to crime and was murdered on the streets in 1920. Frank Worsley, captain of Shackleton's Trans-Antarctic Exhibition's "Endurance," directly entered the British navy upon reaching home after the ice ordeals. A large majority of the twenty-eight survivors of the Expedition volunteered, and two were killed in service. British actors served with the London Scottish Regiment, among them Basil Rathbone, who served in extreme peril as a forward scout, Ronald Colman who was wounded at the Battle of Messines, Claude Rains who suffered a gas attack that nearly blinded him in one eye, and Herbert Marshall, who had a leg amputated. Charles Laughton served in a cyclists' battalion, and suffered gas injuries. The artist Henry Tonks made pastel drawings of facial wounds to be used in surgical reconstructions, and the Vorticist painter Edward Wadsworth served the war by designing camouflage "dazzle" ships for the Royal Navy. Jean Renoir served in the French cavalry, was wounded, and then became a fearless pilot. The "Harlem Hellfighters," the 369th Infantry Regiment, fought from the trenches in the war; they included dancer and actor Bill

"Bojangles" Robinson and jazz composer Noble Sissle. Billie Holiday's father Clarence fought at the very end of the war. After he died of pneumonia in 1937, unattended in the Jim Crow ward of a Texas hospital, Billie suspected that the after-effects of the war's poisonous gas, coupled with white physicians' neglect, hastened his death. The indignities convinced her to record "Strange Fruit," the grim song about lynching that would not have been out of place on the 1914–1918 charnel fields. Maurice Chevalier was wounded, captured, and spent two years in a German prisoner-of-war camp. Albert Camus' father Lucien was killed at the Battle of the Marne in 1914. The intrepid Grand Prix race car driver Georges Boillot was a French forces fighter pilot, killed in 1916 in a dogfight at Verdun-Sur-Meuse. Tour de France champion bicyclist Ottavio Bottechia fought with the Bersaglieri in the Italian army. The surrealist poet and playwright Guillaume Apollinaire's pre-war works were extravagant and visionary; he suffered shrapnel wounds to the temple in 1916, and in a weakened condition, died of influenza two days before the Armistice: may we not imagine that his surrealism was prophetic; that the natural way of the immoral world could be resolved by nothing less than a cataclysm founded merely on ideas of national interest? Pound said that "artists were the antennae of the race." The popular and pioneering French film star and comedian Max Linder served as a dispatch driver between Paris and the front, was wounded and thereafter suffered a devastating depression that led to his suicide in 1925. The brilliant sculptor Rembrandt Bugatti was another sort of casualty of the war; in 1916, disheartened, it was said, by the slaughter of the animals in the Antwerp Zoo, he too committed suicide. A significant number of World War Two's commanding officers had served in the Great War, most notably Erwin Rommel. It is difficult to imagine that his intrepidity and inventiveness were not forged in aggression, in ruined France and Romania.

And only with a profound wonder can one truly appreciate those artists and writers who were killed in the war. The poet Wilfred Owen died 4 November 1918, eight days before the Armistice. H.H. Munro

(Saki) was killed by a sniper at Beaumont-Hamel, aged forty-three; he was insistent upon joining the armed forces as a regular trench soldier. Joyce Kilmer also died by sniper's bullet, at the Second Battle of the Marne in 1918, his strong Catholic faith undiminished by what he saw in the war. The charismatic and preternaturally handsome Rupert Brooke (a lapsing atheist and socialist) died of sepsis on his way to Gallipoli, having already achieved fame for his many war poems. Another war poet, Isaac Rosenberg, was killed in 1918, yet another of the British literati who condemned the war from the beginning, like Briffault, but who felt entirely compelled to join the armed forces. Arthur Graeme West was another pacifist who fought in the war; he was killed by a sniper's bullet at Bapaume in 1916; West's posthumous book was titled The Diary of a Dead Officer. T.E. Hulme, the British imagist poet and critic was killed a quarter mile from where Wyndham Lewis was stationed, in Flanders. They had published work together in Lewis' Vorticist periodical BLAST. He was a friend of Gaudier-Brzeska, a disciple of Henri Bergson, and Pound referred to him as a metaphysician. T.P. Cameron Wilson is best known for the elegiac poem "Magpies in Picardy." He was killed in March 1918. Franz Marc was a painter and friend of Auguste Macke who enlisted in the German cavalry. He was later assigned to create pointillist canvas camouflage to protect artillery installations from airborne detection. Marc was killed at Verdun in 1916. The French cubist sculptor Raymond Duchamp-Villon served in the French army in the medical services, where he contracted typhoid fever. He died of the disease one week before the Armistice, his truncated and unrealized career perhaps suggested by the work of his brother Marcel Duchamp and his friend the printmaker Jacques Villon, both of whom lived and flourished into the 1960s. The artful life of the dashing French-American pilot ace Gervais Raoul Lufbery promised originality and cleverness. Lufbery kept two lions as pets ("Whiskey" and "Soda") when serving with the Lafayette Escadrille, and is sometimes credited with inventing the gin-and-champagne French 75 cocktail; he was shot down in May of 1918. The poet and composer Ivor Gurney was wounded and gassed near Ypres, and, subsequently diagnosed as a paranoid schizophrenic, was institutionalized in a mental hospital for many years afterward. He continued to believe that he was still engaged in battles. Julian Grenfell's poem "Into Battle" is often considered the most anthologized poem of the war, and served to abet the propaganda that encouraged boys to seek glory in war; he wrote: "I adore war. It is like a big picnic but without the objectivelessness of a picnic." Grenfell was killed in May of 1915, before the disillusion that occurred to so many other enthusiasts could temper his views. His younger brother was killed in July of that year. Edward Thomas, the esteemed British poet and literary critic, was killed at the Battle of Arras in 1917, by a concussive blast that showed virtually no outward physical damage, but which caused his heart to stop beating; that effect was not uncommon. The English Poet Laureate Ted Hughes referred to Thomas as "the father of us all." Thomas' deeply allusive writing about the English countryside, derived from a close understanding of the rural scene, will have perhaps seen the destiny of doom in the French and Belgian topographies. We may easily conjecture that some of these writers' and artists' early work had anticipated major works, epics, and perhaps even new genres.

We can imagine writers living after the war brooding on the way in which its horror was ineradicable, and worse, quite natural to cultured societies. T.S. Eliot's 1922 "The Waste Land" does not much mention the war, but cannot be understood by anyone incognizant of the four years of slaughter, the complicit encouragement of an uninformed British citizenry, and a harrowing moral public ambivalence. James Joyce began writing *Ulysses* in 1914 in Trieste and Zurich, the manuscript of apparent incoherence and shattered prose anticipating the early century's theme of things coming apart. Fitzgerald's *Tender Is the Night* reads more like a movie script than a novel, but the paragraph or two set at the Newfoundland Memorial at Beaumont Hamel is a haunting suspension of his storytelling, when fiction just will not serve. Fitzgerald also invented a phrase to describe the way in which the war ravaged the morale and underscored the frailty of humankind: "non-combatant's shell-shock." D.H. Lawrence wrote:

> I suppose you think the war is over and that we shall go back to the kind of world you lived in before. But the war isn't over. The hate and evil is greater now than ever. It makes me sick to see you rejoicing like a butterfly in the last rays of the sun before winter. Hate will be damned up in men's hearts and will show itself in all sorts of ways which will be worse than war. Whatever happens there can be no peace on earth.

Christopher Isherwood was ten years old when the war began, and the conflict coincided with his discovery of the allure of philosophy and his peering into the shadows of his sexuality. We may associate his evolution with the moral appreciation of the tone of life in artistic Berlin in the 1930s, as the brutal German will of the First World War was emerging from its astringent hibernation, exactly coterminous with the era's delightful decadence. Leonard Woolf, too, traveled in Germany in the thirties; he wrote prophetically of both the unresolved spirit of grievance among the German citizenry and their proclivity to act cooperatively. Patrick Leigh Fermor's epic walk from the Hook of Holland to Constantinople, in 1933-1935, revealed to him troubling elements in the German nature, a natural conformity and an arrogance that were beginning to be exploited by Hitler.

Pulp novels published shortly after the war predictably hurled invective upon the Boche and inspired worship of the Tommies, thereby perpetuating the sort of martial fantasies that enabled men to resume regarding war as glorious and heroic. Stanley Kubrick's 1957 movie *Paths of Glory* introduces the genre of modernist skepticism about the war; it remains a focal example of "anti-war" works of art. Though the French army was, in fact, almost ruined by mutinies, the movie's execution of soldiers chosen for emblematical death purely at random for the cowardice and desertion of soldiers they never met accentuated the French High Command's malignant pairing of morale and mortal intimidation. This sentiment of madness had appeared in nucleus form in Howard Hawks' movies *The Dawn Patrol* and *Road to Glory*. In the latter, the nurse Monique asks simply: "What sense does it make just to be brave? Why do you all have to die?" It is not so far from this, as we might wish to hope, to Monty Python and Blackadder, when wrenched logic twisted reason into juxtapositional comedy.

In our own time, some few flickerings have unexpectedly appeared in popular music: Siouxie and the Banshees' "Poppy Day"; Iron Maiden's "Paschendale" [sic]; and Thom Yorke and Radiohead's wailing threnody to the last living veteran.[7] Kevin Puts' 2008 opera *Silent Night* deals in part with the storied Christmas Truce of 1914, when German and British troops met in No Man's Land, their natural hearts having occluded national allegiances (an act deemed treasonous by the authorities). An affinity with the Vorticists is obvious in all these artworks: hard angles, blunt facets and forms, rigid declarations, noise. Subtlety is not associated with the Great War; few books mention long lyrical passages of soft and languid daydreaming. It was a place for clashing, screams, and peril. Percy's "angelism" of the lost self, and Flex's "He who swears on Prussia's flag has nothing left that belongs to himself" are recapitulated in the foreword to the 2014 production of the Met's Prince Igor: "To unleash a war is the surest way to escape from oneself." Bernard Tavernier's 1989 film *Life and Nothing* describes the process of identifying dead French soldiers, and distributing their effects to surviving wives and families. The macabre element resides not in the bodies of the buried corpses, but in the minds of those who are identifying the remains. Jean-Pierre Jeunet's 2004 film *A Very Long Engagement* subsumes the war in the obsessive love and search for a battle-killed fiancé. Exploring potential objective correlatives for a war of nonsense and brutality, the 1966 film *King of Hearts* more obviously places it among the denizens of a lunatic asylum. Sebastian Faulks' 1993 novel *Birdsong* creates another sort of reciprocity by tethering the disease and gore of the trenches with an erotic, illicit passion of a love affair. The 2002 film *Deathwatch* locates Mephistophelian evil itself in the trenches, taking its form in malice and murder and paranormal grotesqueries. The movie is cataloged under the genre "horror film," a reminder that though the setting is the battlefield, and the story may be related as history, the thing was less a geo-political confrontation than the ultimate expression of the darkest slough of men's vanity and malice.

It is in contemporary accounts that we may breathe a moment in the familiar comfort of our own contexts to examine the soul of the war, in our own time's language. *The Missing of the Somme* (2011) by Geoff Dyer, provides the nearest statement we might have to an achronological field theory of war, connecting its lessons to our present lives and our speculative force of mind. Dyer transcends the remorse that informs many lesser latter-day reflections on the war, their obsession with memorialization, and their designated, silent pauses smothered in intentionality. He returns the genre of elegy to its original form, as it had been perfected by Coleridge and Gray. His exposition and contemplation are intensely in the first person. The subtlety of empathy is his first consideration. Dyer and a very few other writers' personalization is set against contemporary histories that tend to replicate the broad, remote view that Sassoon had anticipated. Soldiers died, but we can refresh our point of view by attending to the sorts of spectrums we have been exposed to by, say, African-American Studies Programs, which note that the gathering of severed limbs and heads and the reinterment of hastily buried bodies—an immensely disgusting task—was assigned to American black platoons and colored immigrants. Modris Eksteins writes in *The Rites of Spring* that the modernism foreseen by Joyce, Pound, Stravinsky, and Eliot before the war, materialized after the war, in the twenties, yet other waves of cultural biases gained a footing, including new heights of materialism, the debasement of popular forms of art, and the replacement of one's own aspirations with mediated views of sports heroes and movie stars. As Auguste Villiers de l'Isle wrote in his play *Axël,* "Living? Our servants can do that for us." Empathy is no longer necessary when modern sensibilities can simply observe other lives, cooly, detached; Modernism and Post-Modernism provide the liberation of irony—an outside viewing that provides protection against the insults of corruption.

The First World War was transcendently repulsive, and it helped create new limits of depravity and moral malevolence. New forms of personal expression such as jazz, experimental film, and the bolder visual arts evolved after the war, but also did the pervasive gloom of anger and nihilism that drifted and then slipped into totalitarian fascism and communism, and their paranoid rejection of the creative, degenerate arts. In 1937, Wyndham Lewis wrote:

> The War bled the world white. It had to recover. While it was in that exhausted state a sort of wee-world sprang up and flourished. All that was real was in eclipse, so that all that was unreal came into its own and ran riot for a season. But now the real is recovering its strength.

One element of the years called "post-war" was the need by individuals and societies as a whole to forget. Part of the question being raised by affairs relating to the Centennial is whether or not that absence of mind and forgetting was an obliteration or a mere burying. Lewis again:

> However this is enough about a system of things, which although joined to the Great War by the post-war, is really a distinct division of Time. The Great War is a magnet, the post-war its magnetic field. The war sickness, the post-war is over—we can look back at the first War with fresh eyes. If we don't learn a thing or two from this scrutiny it will be our fault entirely. For it was a particularly silly war, and it is most important if England is to indulge in another war it should not be completely senseless. For that would be the third.

Our own evaluation and feeling for the First World War demands and in some cases creates the need for us to assume ancient moral techniques we may have been encouraged to think we can do without. Empathy can be reborn.

Jaroslav Hašek's 1923 novel *The Good Soldier Švejk* creates and immortalizes the character who might best express the twenty-first century's understanding of a trench war in which artificial boundary lines, nominal affiliations, and moral platitudes and sophistries coalesced into slaughter, depravity, and ruination. Švejk prevails, and in fact eludes physical or psychic damage by means of his oblique ineptitude, his cunning, and his routinely contradicting expectations. Though, in human and cultural terms, the war was the equivalent of the burning of the Alexandrian and Córdoban libraries many times over, the only response to it should have been wonderment or, perhaps, undifferentiated dread about the human condition, but Švejk asserted his individualism and, so far as we can tell from the text, his soul and heart were unaffected by the barbarity. It was all just too mad for him to understand. Similarly, e.e. cummings, in his 1922 novel *The Enormous Room*, neutralizes the possible corrosion of his well-being by converting the war's madness and the privations of his prison cell into personally-relevant presentations of his individualistic interpretation: a charleyhorsed English language, pictographic representation, and his non-historical, idiomatic ways of looking at things. (Such a salvational psychological reframing has not been noted in the literature for men wholly entrenched under fire.)

The post-war zeitgeist revealed—began to reveal—the flowering of satire and black comedy, the resignation of despair, existentialism, subversion of authority, skepticism, hopelessness, and finally, revolt and protest. Despite the oceans of lost lives, the Great War never amounted to anything more than an abortion of the preposterous. Hašek (yet another communist) produced a satire of the blackest comedic form, and it is the best expression of at least one crucial aspect of the Great War: its absurdist madness and folly, the ineptitude and culpability of its leaders, its illogicality, proof that poisonous snakes can indeed swallow their tails, and an epical revelation of Sisyphean ineffectuality. Richard Attenborough's 1969 film satire *Oh, What a Lovely War!* and Richard Lester's World War II spoof *How I Won the War* are significantly indebted to Hašek, and Joseph Heller respectfully acknowledges *The Good Soldier Švejk* as the very first expression of ironic modernism's ambiguous paradox, immortalized as catch-22.

There are hundreds of other statements and beliefs about the Great War, many of which present opposite, or only-heroic views. Bibliographies and catalogs of the written word, photograph and film libraries, and personal collections of ephemera all assure that a permanent record exists and will be maintained. Google Books and Project Gutenberg digitization ventures make available new diaries and artworks, and the Facebook[36] pages "World War One Historical Association" and "WW1-Buffs," among several others, frequently post images and documents from persons in possession of their grandfathers' attic stuffs: letters and photographs never before cataloged or contributed to historical societies; never before in the public record. These are fabulous resources, and such new documentation can bring to light previously suppressed information that might counterbalance stories of bravery, or reveal sexual, moral, and political unpleasantries. At the very least, these revelations will add to the idea that the war is not to be conveyed only by credentialed historians, and that it can instead rely on the primary document of everyman. Yet excepting the activities and visibility attending to the Centennial, the war has vanished from the public discussion. Millions of men listened to the wrongheaded and stubborn platitudes of one hundred men, yet some very few others will not be so easily fooled into brutality. Švejk and Yossarian and other iconoclasts and dissident mutineers live in our world today.

Henri Alban-Fournier (the writer Alain-Fournier) was killed in the very first days of the war, in September of 1914, near the Meuse River and Verdun. His only published work was the 1913 novel *Le Grand Meaulnes*. The book was carried by Sal Paradise in *On the Road*, was loved by Gore Vidal, and is said to have influenced and prefigured *The Great Gatsby*. (Fitzgerald was docked and bound for Europe when Armistice came in 1918.) Alain-Fournier much admired Debussy's opera *Pelléas et Mélisande* (as did Proust) not least for its dreamlike impressionism, as the book renders that same peculiar sort of mysticism that is the most affecting—the kind which may turn out to be real. *Pelléas et Mélisande's* luscious art requires no script or story; its musicality conveys everything Debussy will ever have wanted to say. Alain-Fournier's novel bears a number of resemblances to key features of modernism, and is often associated with Proust, Camus,

Sartre, and Derrida as the vital touchstones of French aesthetic philosophy. *Le Grand Meaulnes* also reminds us of the liberties of youth as they become constrained by the responsibilities of maturity, and by the false standards of previous generations and their likewise inherited strangling regulations. The novel recalls Flaubert, Henri Murger, and George Sand, at the same time as it looks forward to Holden Caulfield and Françoise Sagan's Cécile in *Bonjour Tristesse*, and an encouraging plenitude of other literary outcasts and contrarians. The novel's patterned evocations of transgressiveness, charisma, cool, the transformative vision, and otherworldliness are all familiar conventions of the battlefront experience. *Le Grand Meaulnes* is sometimes revealingly translated as *The Lost Domain*. Alain-Fournier's life was extinguished in eastern France and the conception of his future work vanished, but *Le Grand Meaulnes* reigns as a symbol of man's refusal to be conscripted into events unsanctified by one's own soul.

All of these writers, save perhaps Empey and Mackin, have abjured the "story" or the narrative eventuation of the war, and instead have relied chiefly on written or visual impressions and suggestive metaphorical language to convey the real heart and truth of the catastrophe. In part this is due to the inherent ambiguities of the war—its illogicality, its monumental stupidity—but figurative rather than narrative representations of the effects and impressions of the war may be the only way to convey its true legacy. Stories are often the cheapskate synopsis of the human experience, and plot and narrative cannot do more than sketch the scene for persons who are satisfied with a journalistic or empirical understanding; Brecht referred to the "lowly art of the story." A truer telling requires, instead, a sort of moving x-ray to engage and coalesce intuitive forces that are fundamental to the scope of the war and its damage to the soul, the alteration of the collective reaction to such barbarities, and the implication that cultures are much closer to primitivism than the cultural graces that are suggested by, say, the fine fabrics of Lille. Concerning this war Briffault wrote, "occidental ears await melody in vain."

Harry Patch died in 2009 at the age of 111. He was the last man alive who had fought at Passchendaele.

> When the war ended, I don't know if I was more relieved that we'd won or that I didn't have to go back. Passchendaele was a disastrous battle—thousands and thousands of young lives were lost. It makes me angry. Earlier this year, I went back to Ypres to shake the hand of Herr Kuentz, Germany's only surviving veteran from the war. It was emotional. He is 107. We've had 87 years to think what war is. To me, it's a licence to go out and murder. Why should the British government call me up and take me out to a battlefield to shoot a man I never knew, whose language I couldn't speak? All those lives lost for a war finished over a table. Now what is the sense in that? Irrespective of the uniforms we wore, we were all victims. War was the calculated and condoned slaughter of human beings, too often sent into combat as 'cannon fodder' by politicians who should have settled their conflicts by dueling among themselves. War isn't worth one life. Too many died.

Harry Patch also recalled a mortally wounded soldier in the mud: "'Shoot me,' the young German soldier begged," but before Patch could draw his revolver the man was dead.

> I was with him for the last 60 seconds of his life. He gasped one word—'Mutter—Mother'. That one word has run through my brain for 88 years. I will never forget it. I think it is the most sacred word in the English language. It wasn't a cry of distress or pain; it was one of surprise and joy.

In 1912, Gaudier-Brzeska visited the London Zoo:

> The beasts had a curious effect on me, which I haven't hitherto experienced; I have always admired them, but now I hate them—the dreadful savagery of these wild animals who hurl themselves on their food is too horribly like the way of humans. It's most depressing thus

to see our own origin—depressing, not because we sprang from this, but that we may so easily slip back to it—a big war, an epidemic—and we collapse into ignorance and darkness, fit sons of chimpanzees.

FROM THE ARCHIVES

Research Collection
McMaster University, Hamilton, Ontario, Canada[8]
(Original letters are in the British Library Archives and Manuscripts)

Lawrence Koons and William Hixson conducted interviews and research for a prospective biography of Robert Briffault in the early 1960s. Though they eventually abandoned the project, each unconvinced he could do justice to their subject's extensive intellectual breadth and large life, they were able to meet with many of Briffault's principal acquaintances, only twelve years after his death. Their research materials were eventually donated to the McMaster University Archives, in Hamilton, Ontario, Canada, and include correspondence with Herma Briffault, photographs, plus extensive interpretive notes by Koons composed immediately after his interviews.

It is possible to believe that Robert Briffault regarded the 1209–1229 Albigensian Crusade as the fatal conclusion of humanity's hopes that humankind's spirit of romance might form the first rule of human liberalism and gentility. Instead, as he might have it, heartless marauders astride armored horses slaughtered the serene poets of Provence and Languedoc with the pitiless swords and spears of hatred and paranoia. Pope Innocent III had predicted that his Church could become colossally wealthy in power and gold, and this fond hope was contradicted by the Catalonian-influenced poverty and purity of the Cathars and troubadours. The Moorish and western European glories were largely extinguished by the Pope's Christ-fanatics and by capitalistic usury. But that final form of despotism had not reached its zenith until 1914, when several brands of landed and armied fascists had the hubris to presume that their material and nationalistic desires constituted reason enough to take advantage of tribes they deemed less adequately militaristic. In any case, every tribe was mostly peopled with the insufficiently productive—"they would have had desperate and grim lives anyway"—and they could be fed, almost without surcease, onto broad death.

Briffault's letters to his daughters from Flanders are graphic descriptions of his life in the war. After long narratives about the conditions and horror of the front, he didactically advises them to see *Birth of a Nation*, and *Intolerance*, and to read Swinburne (perhaps for the *épater le bourgeoisie?* or because Swinburne once planned an epic poem on the Albigensian Crusade?). These three particular recommendations may be taken as aesthetic antidotes to nationalism, suborning, and the miserable warmongering crafts of evil in which he was immersed.

Briffault writes to his beloved daughter Muriel from Passchendaele; she is eighteen:

> The country around Ypres must once have been very beautiful. Ypres (a most picturesque old town like Bruges) lies on a flat circle surrounded by an half amphitheatre of low rolling hills. It was a terrible looking battlefield strewn with corpses—English, Australian, German. From there we could have a good view of our objective, the Passchendaele ridge which lies in front. Having taken our bearings we returned under constant heavy shell fire. It was a wet tramp through Poperinghe, Vlamerdinghe, and Ypres to the old German line where we were dumped, and it was the reverse of comfortable. There being nothing there except a mud ditch. We set to gathering pieces of corrugated iron and trench grids and made some kind of cover where we could manage to sit down and eat and sleep. I slept on a trench grid while the Colonel slept on a heap of sandbags. Next day a party of us went out to reconnoitre the ground of our attack.
>
> I am getting quite a lot of cases of self-inflicted wounds—fellows shooting off one of their fingers or putting a bullet through their foot—they say, of course, that their rifle went off while they were cleaning it—but until two or three are shot—as they will be—they'll go

on playing this game to get off. You couldn't grouse and be miserable over it, so you laugh at it—that is the 'smile of victory' which the illustrated papers show you (piffle!!)—it's really a smile of despair.

In England people are disgusted and indifferent as a result of the policy of lies and jingoism which the press—ruled by the military—has ceaselessly carried on since the beginning of the war. Wimbledon is a "masterpiece," the dwelling-place of a well-to-do smug people suffering from complete atrophy of the brain—there is not a discordant note anywhere, everything speaks of heartless English suburbanity undefiled—it appears to be peopled by chambermaids and Sunday-school-teaching shop boys. The girls are rosy-cheeked imbeciles. It is an unpatriotic place, because it makes one pro-German to look at it. Every flame of thought and living feeling is as surely extinguished there as in an atmosphere of carbonic acid.

I established my aid post in one of the larger pillboxes, one, in fact, that had been the German Aid Post. Our communications were practically cut off with the rear and we were isolated in the midst of the wilderness of mud and shell holes. We got, however, an order from the General to "go the whole hog," and about two o'clock in the afternoon we pushed again right to the top of the hill with Passchendaele village two thousand yards in front of us. News trickled through later of the battalions that should have helped us. One had lost their way altogether in the darkness and mud, the other had refused to advance beyond Abraham Heights, where, under heavy shell fire, they had entrenched themselves. So that our battalion was the only one in the brigade that did the work unaided. The cost was, however, terrible. The whole of our position was swept with machine gun fire from the left, and worst of all was the sniping—one couldn't show one's self one minute without being sniped at, and the shooting was marvelously accurate and deadly. My aid post, small enough in all conscience, was soon full of wounded, not only our own men, but those of the brigades on our left and right, for none of their military officers had got up and I had to practically do the medical work of the whole Division. The little bit of concrete place I was in was soon chock-a-block full with wounded—there was not enough room to stand anywhere. The lighter cases had to stay outside and many of them got killed outside the door. The ambulance part of the medical arrangement failed completely, in spite of numerous messages which I sent back, not a single RAMC bearer made his appearance during

the whole of the show (their job being to evacuate wounded from the
Regimental Aid Post to the Ambulance Advanced Dressing Station).
I sent away all the cases that could walk in batches with a guide to
the A.D.S. And later managed to muster a number of stragglers from
one of the battalions that should have helped us and got them to
carry back some lying cases, but the stretchers never came back. It
is terrible work carrying stretchers amid the waste of mud and shell
holes, hard enough to carry yourself, let alone a loaded stretcher. We
had great difficulty, too, in getting our own cases down from various
parts of the field. We organized several parties to collect them but
two of our stretcher bearers got shot, and it is very difficult to find
men in the honeycomb of shell holes, as you may pass quite close to
them without seeing them. We scarcely had stretchers too and after
I had to go and dress the cases as I found them and leave them to be
collected later after giving them some food and drink. Once a man
crawled up to me and said, "Good morning, Sir," and I recognized
the old Mess Corporal that used to be in the 1st York. He once saved
my life (figuratively speaking) by giving me a tin of tongue on the 3rd
of September at Thiepval, and I jokingly handed him a tin of tongue
which I happened to have in my haversack (it was a pleasure to see
him devour it). He had been lying wounded in the leg in a shell hole
for 36 hours. On the night of the 11-12th we were relieved by the 2nd
Otago Battalion of New Zealanders. (There was no one I knew, but
the military officer knew me by name, he was from ChCh, and my
servant told me afterwards that one of the men had asked him if
I was Doctor B.) Our battalion got safely out, but I stayed behind
to see what could be done to evacuate the wounded and also to
look for one of our officers that was missing. I had an exciting time
during the latter job. I finally left at dawn with a small party, crawled
through violent shell fire, lost my way on Abraham Heights but in
the end landed safely at the place near Ypres where the ambulance
was. They were just handing over to the New Zealand ambulance and
the first man I saw was Major Murray to whom I told the situation
and that there were still 44 wounded in the line, and he promised to
go there and put all the New Zealand bearers of the ambulance on
the work, a promise which he kept. Passing through Ypres I found
my groom waiting for me with my horse, I was about done by
then, so I rode on. By the way, I passed a motor ambulance in
front of which was sitting a fat little pig-faced man, and I recognized

Mardie Neil! I found out that our battalion (what was left of it) was entraining for a back area. I hurried to the entraining point, but was only just in time to see the train move off. So I got hold of our Quartermaster who was proceeding later and arranged to go with him. When all was settled I dropped on the ground in front of the tent, thoroughly exhausted. A New Zealand rifle sergeant came up to me and gave me some whiskey and a cigarette and later (when I had quite recovered) came and asked me if he could bring me some tea and food as they were just going to have their lunch. I said, "You'll do nothing of the kind, I'll come and have it with you." So I had my first meal in the New Zealand sergeant's mess. They were Otago men mostly, but the Sergeant Major came from Auckland, from Renivera, he told me (sorry I've forgotten his name). They, being cavalry, had never been in action in France except for a short while at Vincy. I gave them some Boche "souvenirs" I had about me. To make a long story short, I ultimately rejoined the battalion at a place over the border in France. They were worrying considerably about a missing officer (the one I had searched for) and decided to send a party back to look for him again. I offered to take charge and we got away again, borrowing a motor lorry, and got back to our battlefield in the afternoon of the second day after I left it. The New Zealanders who were to have pushed on further, had had an even worse time of it than we did, they could not advance an inch, and they were pretty well wiped out. Their dead were lying in heaps all over the place killed by machine guns. Let me tell you here that there is but one verdict in all ranks here about the New Zealand troops and it is "*The finest troops in the British army.*" Our Colonel is an old fashioned regular, used to be very prejudiced against "your damned Anzacs" as he used to call them to me, but he has completely changed and is the first to speak of them as the "finest soldiers in France." When I got up to our lines there was a kind of truce. On getting up to the top of the ridge I spotted two Boches. Directly they saw us they waved a white flag and pointed to their Red Cross brassards. I signed to them to come up to me, covering them with my revolver, and one hastily came, the other hung back a bit. They also were busy collecting wounded. The Boche told me they had roped in a good many of our wounded but he did not know if there were any officers amongst them. The Boche stretcher bearer carried an automatic pistol (which he had no business to) and I told him to give it up, which he did. I let him go after that as we were both on the same errand, and he went away with "Ach, Es ist ein trauriger Krieg, Herr Offizier." After searching a bit longer we found our wounded and got them back to the New Zealand Aid Post. Murray had been as good as his word and evacuated all our casualties the same day.

We got back without further incident to our camp at Wienriezeele (which I call Venezuela). That was our second battle of Ypres.

After two days rest we were chucked into our third. First we were dumped in a field in front of Ypres. The Boche planes came over at dawn and we had to strike our tents at dawn most unpleasant. In spite of the precautions they came on the last morning we were there and dropped bombs all over us killed 10 of our men and wounding 14. Our next battlefield was on another part of the ridge, near Zonnebeke. The difficulty of getting there was the same as ever. We suffered heavily from intense shell fire on the way and getting there at dark, I had difficulty finding my quarters. They are the most terrible quarters I have ever occupied. Not a comparatively large fortified farm like the last, but a real pillbox. That is a concrete structure with about 6 feet of solid concrete on the top and a thick concrete wall facing west and a thin one facing east. If you had seen the prisons on Venice, those they call the Pozzi, you would wonder how human beings could exist in them. (A rat hole four feet high and five foot square.) Well, my rat hole in the pillbox was even worse, the dimensions were the same, but the floor was a quagmire a foot deep, indescribably filthy water which I described as 60% of dead Boche. For another compartment of the pillbox occupied by three dead Boches separated from us only by a wooden partition open at the bottom, soaking in the same water. We crawled over stepping stones of petrol tins and forming two ledges on which one lay. It was impossible to sit up or to lie full length. There I dwelled for four days and five nights! The dressing of the wounded was, of course, done altogether outside. While we were there we were continuously subjected to the worst German bombardment I have experienced, our guns were too far back and the Boche ones too far forwards and tremendously strong. It was just what it must have been before Verdun at is worst. It was one continuous crash of shells in all directions. My unfortunate pillbox was a favourite target. While I was there, it was hit five times plumb on the top, but the six feet of concrete stood firm, though when I left it, it was chipped and badly cracked and I'm sure it has not stood much longer. On the second night my bearers and servants were sheltering under railway sleepers outside a kind of lean-to we had built up. One shell hit it sideways and wounded my servant in the neck. They all had to be got inside as best as possible. We were seven in all. Two hours later a terrific crash took place, our candle went out and there were terrified screams. A shell had landed exactly at the door of the rat hole and blown right inside. When I had brushed the mud and muck off my face and told everyone to keep perfectly still, I got my flashlight out of my pocket and amid the mass of writhing and groaning humanity ascertained that my Sergeant (who has been my right hand for close to a year) was hit through the body and a corporal had a compound fracture of the thigh. Another man was killed outright. You may, or rather you cannot imagine the job it was to dress the two wounded men in such a hole. We had to get them on to the planks that served as ledges and performed feats of contortions on top of petrol tins! That night was beyond comparison the most ghastly night I have ever spent. Cramped in the most back and limb-breaking position between two wounded men who were calling constantly on me to hold their hand or give them a pull out of my water bottle, holding a candle in one hand, as there was no other place to put it, breathing a pestilential atmosphere that turned one's stomach, nothing was wanted to complete the horror of that hell. And the shells came dropping again and again on our heads and we wondered how long the roof would hold out. I looked at my watch and followed the slow creeping of the hours—1, 2, 3, 4, 5—at last came 6 o'clock and dawn. At that hour the Boche, having made sure that no new attack was coming, usually slowed down his shelling for an hour or two, it was the breathing time of the day. We managed after infinite labor to dig ourselves out of the choked entrance; to drag the wounded men out and to carry them to the Advanced Dressing Station. I spent three other nights in that place, but nothing approached the horror of that night. Being to a great extent cut off from the rest of the battalion, I didn't hear until the morning of the 23rd that relief had taken place, by a Canadian battalion. At dawn on the 23rd I set off with the remains of my staff and a few stragglers that we collected at the Aid Post. As luck would have it, a new Canadian Battalion had been picked up and was strafing the Boche, so instead of the morning peace, we got retaliation from his guns. But we were desperate and ploughed our way through the mud and shell holes disregardful of the barrage. At one spot, near the new Canadian battery, it was terribly intense and we thought that we could not possibly escape. Shells were bursting all around us, back, front, right and left. I felt a sharp pain in my right leg and thought I had a blighty but the splinter only tore through my puttees and stockings and merely scratched my leg; another shell splinter lodged in my left hand. Out of breath we reached a large dugout, that of the Canadian gunners, and paused to get our breath. Then we proceeded and at last reached the Ypres road. The setting of all these happenings is a waste of shell holes reaching as far as the eye can see in every direction; the whole of it strewn with corpses; it is difficult enough to look after the wounded, it is out of the question to look after the dead, and consequently they lie everywhere, friend and foe, their mud-stained clothes with poor grey faces and hands blending with the mud of which they seem a part. And everywhere dead horses, for one of the hardest jobs is to bring up rations and ammunition and the horses that are used as pack animals perish by the hundreds under the shell fire; others get drowned in the mud. I passed two whose eyes haunt me still. They were alive, but only their heads above the ocean of mud. I stopped a moment to put a revolver bullet through their heads and put them out of their agony. Men too, too hopelessly wounded to be removed frequently call out to one to shoot them and end their misery; I gave several a poisonous dose of morphia, the only thing I could do for them.

Briffault provides another view of these experiences in his novel *Europa in Limbo*:

Julian walked back over the broken ground. The sun had just set. From the high ground the whole land sloping down to Ypres could be seen. The silhouette of the ruined Cloth Hall tower was distinguishable on the horizon against the red sky. The eye ranged from the flooded country of the Yser in the north to the heights of Kemmel and Mont des Catts in the south. Never probably had human eye looked before upon such vastness of desolation. Over the whole prospects was not one leaf or blade. Mile after mile the earth stretched out black, foul, putrescent, like a sea of excrement. Not a sign of animal or vegetable life; none of human life either, for it hid itself underground, and only the dirt spouts thrown up by missiles of death, bursting like mephitic bubbles over the foulness, gave visible indication of its presence. But everywhere the detritus and garbage of the murderous madness. It was one vast scrap heap. And, scattered over or sunk in the refuse and mud, were the rotting bodies of men, horses, and mules. Of such material was the barren waste that stretched as far as eye could see. It was not a desert of nature, a waste land of rock or sand, but what had lately been a fertile and smiling landscape, green and luxuriant, peaceful and pleasant, covered with waving fields, pastures, gardens, orchards, strewn with villages and farms. It stank, lurid and blasted in the poisoned air.

Julian, with Inglis, Sergeant Trutton, Sergeant Day, and Corporal Shortable, took up his quarters for the night in a "pillbox" on the Zonnebeke railway line. They crept through the low opening into the cylinder of concrete. A narrow ledge ran around three sides of the interior. The middle of the pillbox was a pit filled with greenish black water from which rose an intolerable stench. "There's two dead Germans in there," Corporal Shortable informed.

All five sat on the concrete ledge and a couple of planks laid across the stinking water, taking turns stretching out their legs.

Outside the storm of shellfire grew fiercer as the night darkened. It was unceasing. Only the shells that burst quite near were heard as separate explosions against the continuous roll of the tempest. Some burst just outside the pillbox. They alternated with crumps which sounded a few hundred yards away. Two guns were firing at intervals of three minutes at the two pillboxes on the lower slope of the ridge, the one in which the men were sitting and the other, some five hundred yards further on.

"Come in, you runners, we can make room," Julian called to the men outside.

"We're all right sir. We're in the lee. The crumps drop on the other side," Lance Corporal Beddoes called back.

The five men sat in silence, in dull, stupid silence. They've got the range exactly. Then another on the next pillbox. Three minutes, another still. It must have hit the corner. The whole place shakes and rocks. One can hear the crumbling cement. A direct hit and all will be over. Three minutes. That one dropped a bit short. The next crash has hit the roof. Julian feels as though he has been struck on the head. The pillbox quivers and creaks. Another direct hit will finish it. Like that one they passed coming up, with the four German gunners. They will look like that. They will be all mixed up with the two dead Germans in the greenish black water. It is inevitable. The five men sit, saying no word. There is nothing worth saying. Corporal Shortable lights another candle from the stump of the one which has burnt out. They sit waiting for the next crash. Will it be the last?

Julian did not feel afraid. He asked himself whether he was afraid. No, it was curious, but he really did not feel afraid in the least. He felt terribly uncomfortable, and weary. But not, as far as he could make out, afraid. It was the end. There could be no doubt about it. It was not a question of chances this time. The German battery was deliberately aiming at the pillbox, and they had the range exactly. Had it on their map. It was their job, to smash that pillbox, if they took all night to do it. Question of mathematics. Damned poor gunnery, by the way, that they hadn't yet made a job of it.

Well, it had to come. The sooner it was over, the better. It was the waiting in the condemned cell that was nerve-racking. Julian's mood and thoughts had none of the solemnity appropriate to the occasion. Considering this was his leave-taking of life, of the world, the last moments he would spend in this world. Inevitably. None of the drowning man's retrospect. Was it necessary, all this solemnity? No thoughts to rethink. He had thought pretty well all his thoughts to a dead end. Life? He had, after all, had as good a life as most people and a better one than many. There was not much to regret. He had often been very foolish—like everybody else. But he had come to see things pretty clearly, he had grown out of the Days of Ignorance. That was what he valued most in his life. He would have liked to live to see how things would come out of this crucial crisis, this turning point in the growth of Europe, of humanity. That was the chief reason that he had to regret that he had to die now. What was the date? Seventh of November, 1917. He wondered what was going on in Russia, whether the dreams of the man he had met on the Wengern Alp would come to anything. And, over there in Petrograd . . . How was she faring? So many partings of separate lives! Death was only another parting— much like the others. There was nothing to be done about it. If only the gunners would get on with their job, and be done with it. It was intolerable, this waiting. The shell-bursts were now all very near, just missing the rocking, cracking cement pillbox, or grazing it.

Every three minutes. Now. That one dropped a little beyond. Three more minutes. Nearly got it that time. There was a crumbling of cement. The red light of the candle trembled, and nearly went out.

Then it happened. An instantaneous, fulminating crash, stunning, deafening.

It was some seconds before he was aware of what had happened. During an appreciable duration of time, consciousness was obliterated. There was complete silence. That candle had gone out. Darkness and complete silence. Julian became slowly conscious that, as far as he could tell, he was all right. No sound or movement was to be heard in the silence that followed the deafening explosion. No one said a word. Corporal Shortable began fumbling for a match. Then, in the darkness, Sergeant Day gave a low groan, and began whining in a childlike voice, "Oh, my God! I'm hit. Oh, my God!"

When Corporal Shortable had got the stump of candle lit, Sergeant Trutton was nursing his right leg, groaning and complaining. "It hurts, it hurts awful!"

Julian ran his hands quickly over Sergeant Trutton's leg, and tested the bones. The thigh-bone cracked and moved disjointedly as he handled it. The sergeant kept whining like a child.

Sergeant Day lay back with eyes closed, groaning. "For God's sake give me some opium. I can't bear it." Julian and the corporal, who was holding the candle, undid the sergeant's clothes. They could find no wound.

"Where's the pain?"

Sergeant Day pointed to his groin.

There was a tiny wound on the groin.

"Give me some opium, for God's sake."

Inglis sat without saying a word. Julian and the corporal got the two wounded men stretched out on one of the ledges and over the boards. It left very little room for the others to sit.

They bound Sergeant Trutton's leg to a rifle, and he was quiet, saying he felt better. Day was groaning and kept asking for more opium.

"May I hold your hand, sir?" he asked. Julian held the large, rough hand of the sergeant. The physical human contact comforted him. The conventional separation of rank and class was almost bridged.

"What were you in civil life?" Julian asked.

"Foreman in Mr. Foster's factory. Captain Foster's father, you know," said the sergeant. "A very kind gentleman is Mr. Foster. Was good to the workmen. It was a lovely speech he made when the battalion left for France."

Ye Gods! The hallucination of the servile mind!

Night Thoughts
of a World War I
Medical Officer

At Passchendaele the mud was oceanic.

Cries of death came ceaseless as the rain, blowing over Flanders, and
men thought they must be only the slightest bit cleverer than beasts of
burden directed to butchering.

There was work for Briffault, the surgeon,

scouring his hands, eating, and odd moments between—and there was
the dour and obscure state of mind that took the place of sleep.

    And so, do call it sleep, for it was his dreaming.
As in the hold of the clipper knifing through the waves in torment, the
sound of horses and mudsucked-boots,

    wet, cold, during which sentiments half from his heart bloomed
    and formed
    the notion of a sentimental reverie . . .
    . . . *Carlotta entered the patio of the cafè,*
      looking as usual like a million dollars . . .
Fright reduced his dream and force of peers,

other medics, other carriers, other savages minced and unbreathed.

Over the fields of golden mud and creeks a thousand thousand men
sailed like kites their fondest memories back to Germany and Austria
and the British dominions, willing their hands to the domestic table
with family; every man teleported his conversation to such a scene, and
blessed his own presence among the fleshes most familiar.

But here: only lowering fogbanks of gas.

And soon some would learn that those were tables they detested for
their pallid feints of striving, and only back in the mud would they
ever after crave the unequivocal simplicity of living, if even in horror.

    Briffault stays at his table, snipping free a tendon; twisting free the
gristle, and stanching a variety of flows.
Here he learned the blessedness of presence.

One might walk on the basketweaved lines of telepathy over the
canyons and ravines of mud,

    men desiring to be anytime but then—in the inviolable present
    tense . . . that will have happened . . .
in the chilling reality of place-in-dreams that exceeds its own summons.

Crash and sirens, concussive thumps, concussive red and stately
plump, a fabric overlays the men on mud,
hunger, cold, and madnesses speckle the landscape with dread as if the
rays of light were needles of evil

flung above these stillborn descendants of Arthur and Woden,
flattened corpses flatten the sleepers,

lit by the cannons' shimmer,
as miniature waves form patterns of zephyred traces on the brown
pools ubiquitous and drear;

mustard gas on shallow ponds,

resembles both bile and rainbow.

A boy from Manitoba,

a soldier the paperwork names Martin,

   hath ventured onto peril,
     abused and demeaned.
In the sepulcher trench he pressed the palm of his hand against the
wall of mud. Revetment. Firing-step. Parados. Artillery, cannon,
shrapnel.

It might have been called the whole world,

a complete and pure horizon of vista and malaise; sweat during these
episodes wetted against the dried film of mud, and the shuttered eye
did not blunt the bawdy limbs handled and swaddled in black, or in
the catacombs the vestments of washèd sheets.

Clippers and schooners planed across steppes and transvaals, sunrises
and sunsets an astrological clockwork

   beating the drumrhythm of heartbreak,
and casting seeds of Brits who never sailed to Paris Uluru,
meistersingers, bohemian bohunks Catholic Slavs,

   but delivered them onto trenches.

The sublime casque, memory arched, a dove, white as lilies, feathering
below the never-ending note of silence, and the pitiful scenes in dry
rooms,

a golden sound a teacup tapped

and rung by engravèd spoon.

And Lucy nurses souls and amputees.
She reached across the darker woes to tease out of unbridled Martin
the geste of recollection, the peace of divinity, her *drudaria*.

Briffault spake.
Briffault spake in reverie:
Her red lips lay on Martin harmony and flight, his shoulder shaked,
and indefinite bows roosted home the casing swung and blown within,
heaved by Cathars, sprinkled with reds and bubbled pinks, the piercèd
instant turned to Flanders air sunlit.
Death only and alone the goal of civil leagues,

all the teeth had to grind were the particles of death rent and bullied
as by wolves darting, scuttling the sledges of indifferent angels, craning
the specks of so-soft-to-the-touch was this mud, this mud is mine! My
place in the world to caress the skin of the hands of my beloved,

> soft earth and drops of rain mince the skine, and ever hight the
> microline.

Rashers and scalpels, carts of wasted trances dear, follow the road west
yonder onto long prairies of wretchedness akin aloft and besotted, ye
might just heave thyself aboard and save the victims their undignified
yet muted trial.

> Riven souls in bandages cried,
> torrents of mud slurry and bloods coursed as they will and as they
> would,
> forgiven their flooding the deltas, merged as by alchemist's blunt
> formula,
> bereft new oversouls dark in the buttered wounds wept, unmercied
> 'pon the scarrèd lands of Flanders rent and crisped with scabrous
> flakes
> dried in the rains' arbors;

torn spirits sop the cottons bespeaking murmurs lay back for
reposeful
achievement,
men in such rags cake in the rearward black field of aching woe,
touched by the fingers of Beatrice, Laura, and Melisande.
O! might Callisto pine, and ever hight the microline!

The sheets are washed and washed again, once again, and once again,
to enwrap displacèd gores,

misshapen skins,

the flaming rags and bones,

this heart goes still,

while other boys await the dawning of dawn's first light, by which
means of transport

   this one will perish
   and this one will see supper,
   and this one will only know of living
   the grasp and grief of absent clemency.
Three sorts of souls afried and poached,

and slurried on the table meal.

In the trench with his hand 'gainst the wall of mud, Martin is alone
'mid thousands of machines, thousands of munitions, thousands of
holes, he is not the only living creature in this trough; his mind is on
the birds alight zinc-topped bars in Brussels, bunnies of the wood have
walked on, crying

this year in Jerusalem!,

and the trout in the river have joined the herrings, screaming.

Crowds of men hard close by couldna keep him warm or dry.

His riven soul whispered its execration, and knew this much of theatre.

The land was low, and the wide flood covered Passchendaele, one day to glisten blue for ghosts,

a pond of living, a sea of peace,

with currents for the fellowship of men and dogs.

Martin remembered Manitoba,

roasting that morning's trout over the fire;

he had never seen anything so beautiful as its fight, that sunrise; he saw no reason ever to leave that place.

Ye shall know them by their falling, by the slant, by the barrows,

ye shall know them as they sing, as they chant, cordwoods fagots bundles, creaking through the narrows, back to the woodlands, split with fares embalmed; crews to bury, platoons to rearm;

they are identified by fear or peace, packed apace.

Bleak despond and roiling gut,

the hollow eyes, the throat clenched raw to dust, this hand that follied trout in Eden's garden

is all the world ever knowing,

and all the world shall ever know of Being.

And the perfect memories of warm afternoons, this hand of prairie, icy lake, baptized now in molten earth, this handshake, this caress, this rain;

this hand is seen, pressing flat 'gainst glistening mudwall trench.

The fiddler's fingers scattered by grenade

slithered as vermin serpents do,

a drum of fingers holds too the rain,

bits of boneflesh and nail grew anew

in white and black molds,

this new beast stirs,

engenders rather a sort of soul,

a malefactor oily in the alleys,

> naked and greasy an apparition in the coppices' shadows there too
> screaming men lie alive
> and screaming men lie dead.

This gift, that promise.

Fathering and fatherhood denied,

stillborn in the dressings howled;

peeled from shredded skins of merchants,

the shredded muscles of planters,

the broken gritted teeth of Judes fair across the fields, these scarlet
cherries' sogged acart,

spontaneously generate a foetid soul,

cleft to form the memories of soldiers dying alone decades hence,
pitying its consciousness, faithful for its killing, these soft wet grounds

where forests used to tower.

You will know them by their amputations,

know them by their bloods.
    Men who drowned in shellhole pools were declared dead by cheese
        merchants, and were lifted into the handcarts with hard-learned
        indifference by pacifist boys from Bowditch.
Upon these new blood-moors souls spoke of visions, tied by tourniquet
and lash, heaving against which the flesh gave itself up with a squeak,
far through dying onto silences and growls,

a new poach of organmeats positioned themselves for another
dominion of glory, a kingdom of heathened deliberations wicked in
the meal of wormy orchards, rotted along the Menin Road, pock of
mortars' vile breath.

Trains crossed Manitoba and Alberta and Saskatchewan.

Trains routed round the world.

From the Hebrides lads plied Caribbea and Africa.

South of the coast, skiffs in the sunshine turned to port.

What thou lovest well remains: harboring streets and taverns, bingeing
of the linen frail, courtly strollers grailest prail.

Upon these blooded moors waves of stout fellows tramped, knelt in
mires dire,

gritted and clenched,

ligaments taut,

their consciousness a kind of charleyhorse,

a singing out of crampèd spasms.

The buriers buried, fiddler's grim,

the dying dead, glory sucked to quicksand,

then are lost, then forgotten, then rebuked.

They had not known so many had been undone, for the "lost" were
replenished right and by,

in ceaseless devotion, trinkets barreled,

like larks emancipated filling the broad black billow of sky.

Mortars and grenades,

xylyl bromide, phosgene fires boiling skin and sweat, by plan and plot,
voracious for belligerence and for land, any land.

Sodden England said: let a million dead kill a million one.

Attrition is mutual siege, otherwise thought of

as the lakes and ravines and hills and meadows of earth with deer and
rabbits, and not a person known.

Seepage in the trenches drowned

the heartless and the wounded.

The Algerian conscripts fighting with the French wondered broad
what they were fighting there.

Black bread and rum, potato, bacon bullied beef, gristle and tea, fuel
for crematoria, mess for mass graves.

For those who carried their fortune towards another day, dawn comes
with a dismal grey groaning.

Soon the sky will pink and grey,

a fire warms the stage;

his boots during a moment of drowsiness slipped down the mud into
the trench's sewer, whose oily water lapped and filtered to his
cancerous toes.

Dawn will come soon, and a moment of remembrance.

We muds awaiting are dear for valing German men and Boche
boychiks mud-caked cold and anemic.

Streams of tiny roots before his eyes (with rocks and clay, with shale
and slurry of mineral gem),

his hand lifted a finger to touch the nave,

murderous in our cathedral,

he spots the tip of his nose and the arch of his lips with an ointment
of the chalice.

Always a sheen of dust and gravel in the kreel,

as if the perch there spied himself the snake and bear and yon event
true the fisher too.

Martin seemed to have recalled a dream he may have had, in which
instructions were laid out before him on a table, and in our
sacramental privacy he must pull such awful hawsers closer to his
arms and hands, and then, he guessed, they would emerge together as
brothers from the womb, and wade into the mean and spiky measures
of work and woeful woe.

He made the vision, the phantasm of a ship,

creaming waves,

laying to the lines for the bollards silver,

crewmen scrambling for the shore, and leave,

> and rabbit holes, the glass bar of blackwood.
> Smoother than the touch of his finger on the mud wall was the
> black wet scope of vanity.

Cape or bay rounding,

the ship of his dreams painted itself green with delight, its sails the
white soft canvas of billowed cream, whipped with gracious kitchen
sticks,

tied like a fowl for ovens time with cord and cable, golden dolls of
stanchment and security,

aboard the ship the cups of whiskey tossed across the spray, and in the
holds dark couples lay.

The singing stops.

Leaving the harbor in Canada,

rats debarked the ship for public houses

whorehouses

and immediately the snows of an earlier winter, before the plains of
peace descended upon every soul in Alberta, and lay in each soul's
blood and breath, the equanimity of gravity, of forgiveness,

and of one song sung,

played, unified in a thousand hearts as are brewed such streams of
stone-pured marching
> to the great lake where ferries burned and sank and made mad

carnage of villages and families.
   But this dread-fashioned gutter of spit and bloods mingled night
      runs foul as pestilential dying scuttling plagues,
and rot runs wet across the skin and ever toward the wound of black
hole centered and achieved,

dear severance serving the black heart of men mad-possessed.

In the evening three anglers gathered sticks for the fire, and collected
from their rucks black pans and brute cutlery, and whiskey and
cigarettes.

Unformed thoughts became real dreams in the falling toward sleep,
and he remembered from the very distant and lost blackened past
that in the nearest future might they not commit themselves to sacred
injury, such as tortured bodies silent whitened the sky with fears and
faith, faithless frights of bloods in the pans,

snapping in the rock fire,

cleansing as eagles the canyon,

the woods, and house might wish.

They were whalers, shipped to unnavigable waters, bound to the vessel,
fires for the madness' calming,

promised to the maid who would guide them free faultlessly free in
faith to the coast of Brasil.

Before the light, he saw hearts shredded in the solace, rains of beakers
and bottles slopped as they would, canvassing legions of boys and men,

counties plagued and ever lost,

pouring together as if by charnel's wooded troughs, cardinally
murdering discretion panted cross the compass to tear down men and

boys,

boarding ferries together, discussing football,

their harms and cuts balmed and sewn,

leaving for Oostende,

the coast, a harbor, a punt to a faire with bright and laughing girls,
forgotten the piercèd prick,

the bayonet-splitted tongue,

the vast pock of pointless bitter death called large against the sky, the
throngs who came to coliseum half-loving themselves the tigers and the
bears, the gathering of legions in Flanders fields.

The poetic heart tells tall tales,

snuffing the shrieks and burying the eyes in scarves; there is no ready
vision for such loss as this,

and no break or crack appears in the space between the hands of the
arms outstretched, cringing, clenching, and reaching out;

faint through the rustling morning birds he can just hear the screams
of the ultimate supplications,

the whimpering,

the abjection of blood rushed through the tell-tale heart's weeping.

First light pends,

when running from artillery

they turn the mud to diamonds,

and wonder the loss of years no more.

Shrouded and embalmed voices made but to scream from their fair drowning;
stillborn muted and unheard,
cherishing their homes and at one with gravity, light, and word: with
a thin black wand male benignity crackles starlight, a fleet of sailboats
pink 'pon blue Mediterranean lawn, unattributed new oversouls rent
hearts bound yet to earth, and wailed upon Passchendaele hails of
horror no rains might wash away.

In far green dooryards, children twirled,

and dog chased bunny, and Lucy lay her red red lips upon his neck,
today we saw a lady bouqueted by chrysanthemums and fragrance, and
we could scarcely believe how much it altered her imagination in my
opening eyes

   upon muds aflail and frozen suffocation of dawn's very first light
   on tongues.
Scoundrels befouled, not all our combat here,

though aye we have stocked meadow and pond with flanks and
forepaws succulent and dripping a myrrh of valor and keen tenderness,
these snakes and rats bitter bemoan and despoil the golden lads, heave
bulls 'pon the dinner prayer spread.

Too they perish, in brimstone and sulphur,

hanged on barbed wire,

ticks of the clock not otherwise distinguished from the merry and
audacious, stars flicker cross the sky.

If you are dead, stay dead,

ye be villain, ye be prince.

It were better to be eaten alive by bears

than be scoured to nothing by the perpetual motion of a theory of attrition.

Soldiers cold in tight wrappings, prepared for marching west and east, tidal waves receding from the earth,

their soul's self-same song forms a band

and broaches the lands in which their bloods' allure, eventually regaining its own name,

claimed their desire,

and dancing so bold as to make of embraces a sun's brilliant ring.

This amphitheatre, an ocean of mud, an ocean of expanse, the very place of heaven's reach and roll.

Tramping copseward;

heartchambers loft by gusts of surprisèd air,

this is not a moment for remembering,

not a moment for forgiveness,

not a time for resting,

nor an instance of long and generous views of history.

In advance of which a hundred silent sicknesses taste fresh in the breeze, the radiant flame peeked,

in full sun see plain the velts, plains, and valleys of rubies, diamonds, and rivers of silver, rivers of gold.

Secrets even from the conscience scurried,

lost themselves in brambles,

and rotted foul the soil.

Here was calmed the soul,

    nigh the beating heart unhurries itself with rook, pike, and
        flatbread, whiskey and dreaming make caresses,
and sweet accords of pulse and apparition.

Here rocks ringed fire, flamed the pike,

    and doom aged and found itself self-converted
    into the loss of wit and apprehension,
the black interiors ever, and ever, and forever surrendered.

    First Ypres, Second Ypres, Third Ypres:
the transcendental soul is birthed in bowls,

then comes to rest in beauty and peace within these young men.

Then is run like a frantic hare through brambles coarse and alleys
narrow, sizzled 'pon the straws and stones,

and wrought into something that looks very much like a plaited
challah.

Set aside, honey charmeth the soul with desire, the feast of war
gathereth muses and grooms,

and self-hating dreams the matchmen razed, in full.

Sprite! The melancholic guignol,

shrieks from dungeon drear far and black below.

Following the quiet desperation of prophesied boredom on the
meadows of England, young dreams harden like pellets to stones of
surrender, and then in the pits of Flanders,

    are reconstituted by a slime of sea,

as we pour our boys into sieves.

Ton upon ton of Chloride Lime;

sheaths for bodies, time and time again,

the spillage caked in seepage, clung to boots and puttees.

Splinters rotted where had reposed the cherry trees agrove.

But men will hail men on the streets, as they ha' done since street first was formed.

Slitting ope the bags, they didna close the corpses' eyes, for hard by soldiers sneaked lifeless hollow stares.

"This Aussie arrived without his legs.
He asked me straight: 'was I going to amputate?'"

At least he has a face,
which hundreds don't,
yet live.

But the next came next, and after next another, and then we had not known we were so strong, to withstand the worst that men can do and always are.

English men; German men.

Yet when the London stretcher-bearers
met Berliner stretcher-bearers in No Mans Land to rake the earth of corpses and
parts of corpses,
they visited easily with one another,
exchanged cigarettes and conversation.
This was a circumstance that resulted in chits from the chateaux,

forbidding fraternization, forbidding trade, and forbidding the
smelling of flowers,
if flowers were to bloom once more.

"Done. Out." Quoth Surgeon Briffault, time after time.

Forward (hie) and to the left (toward the sea)

and to the right (toward the highlands) hanged feet above the frosted
soils of mud and greasy damp, a mist refracted and diffused by coming
sun,

the grey rainbow of a thousand dull dusky spectrums, beneath which
young men felt their hearts become hollow and their tender loins
faint, dripping into sea amire,

a greying for remembrance,

a grayling on the salver,

grey water tea,

and a crust of bread.

In the distance gulls lowered above the hissing rats who gorge on
putrefying flesh yclept English,

and putrefying flesh yclept German,

the despondent acts of love were like commissions, stanched traffic,
the digging of cesspools, and any number of woes of boredom and
relief in that other place.

The bitterest recognition of an ocean of bitterness, always the corpse
summoned without aforethought or violation or wicked shell,

but the mortal grimace of surprise and indecision.

In six days, one hundred fifty yards of fingers clutching east cost twelve thousand men their final breath and sluice of blood.

Many were undone, and shook like slain chickens, packed in trains for
Ostend; their survivors only grew further into their dear trench, fogs
and rains above like counterpanes of assurance, one massive field of
splintered trees and pockèd vlatenland, the ANZACS, the French, the
Germans, the English; a family of children, cousins napping through
the late afternoon of the europafamily picnic.

Let us say a few words about shell-shock.

It could not be measured, and its existence could never be positively
certified, at least to the satisfaction

of boards in London.

Its duration was uncertain.

    It was known as the thousand-yard stare.
    It looked like fear; exhaustion;
panic and stampede. It looked like drowning,
hysteria, and trembling.

    Its horror is asphyxia, coma, and anesthesia.
    The autopsy of the pickled frog.
Men fought for the crown from 1914 to 1918, and then were executed
for "desertion," which is to say, having been broken into rancid meat,
venomous blood, rasping breath, and uncontrollable trembling.

They said the mud was like a sea.

A few words, then, about the Flanders mud:

it was heavy; its constituent parts include the sewage-shit of a million
men and animals,

and the oils of mustard gas,

stagnant water,

the sour oils of dysentery,

and the floodwaters of despond.

These are the fattest rats zoologists will ever study.

Bloated and made indolent by fleshes. Ten million rats, a thousand million fleas.

Rats unafraid of bombs

stroll up to corpses for sup, insouciant.

Horses and dogs wore gas masks; caked; convulsed; dead.

May we think of menu? Hearty footballers, shopkeepers, farmers, quarrymen.

Platoons communicated with flags (flagmen: I am right here, shoot me now).

Runners against the horizon were perfectly lit (shoot me running).

Cyclists (clay pigeons: strafe me, lend me grenade shrapnel now).

Hundreds of bagpipers were killed (leading the infantry, unarmed, exquisite targets).

Forlorn Hopes: term of art: soldiers at the head of the assault, first doubtless to die.

In the morning, Martin is gathering sticks for the fire (in Manitoba), ringed stones embraced the sacred flame of breakfast, a rasher, fresh milk, hallowed eggs, consecrated rice, and then to catch notice of aside,
as of a dream one may once have had,

the breakfast toast,

braided in gold and speckled with a holy drip of maple syrup, baked bold and pure,

    the transubstantiating breakfast bread,
    but with the pike and the salt of salmon on his lips still, he
    crouched into a fetal ball
clenched shut his eyes,

and named the breads he knew

(mid th' wondrous splashing riot of colors red and orange, a cobalt, a sort of green, a sort of yellow, a sort of amber, a sort of pink) then a coburg, a panettone, baguette,

brioche brown, foccaccia, Irish soda.

When he opened his eyes an arm lay close by,

separated from its golfer,

from its orchardman,

from its cop,

from its farmboy,

treated, as by hasty running men:

crusted blood and crusted mewling stenchèd gore, a rip of spike,

and within the white cotton wrappings,

the breath of a kiwi spirit formerly blue and green, once cried out, and then was hushed and still.

The riverbed in summer crisped,

where once cascades howled aloud their course, and flowed to
gunwales,

flowed to the gutter,

and in the channel creek of stench and reek,

as by some magician half-obscured,

birthed crooked weak and bitter oversouls,

from the slashes leaked,

never forgiven in Flanders' butchered fields.

Lilacs last blooming

show themselves forth as wet and black,

a morbid pulp of gardens defiled,

mulching for broad-reaching acres,

ribs and femurs, clavicles and wrists arisen,

stars in the black sky night of our new home,

silage and loam, fertilizing the lilacs last blooming.

Gores and angels' filmy flakes twinkled in the light, then like leaves fell
in figure eights toward the befoulèd sward, trickled onto a tempered
and impersonal earth, the study of which, in academies far away,

yielded nothing of the hollow eyes men carried, or their minds' swirl-
ing descent

    into General Sir Douglas Haig's and General Charteris' corrupt,
befouled, and mutant incentive of malignant sophistries.

Mongerers of war,

ravens of blood,

the fearsome rule of a thousand snakes

serving soulless earth-bound boors.

    Over the fields of golden mud and gusty bristles a thousand
        thousand men sailed souls from trench to trench to trench,
stopping to tarry but a bit on surgeon's table, or slipping off to
another home, to beefsteak and pie, or to the discovery and
connoisseurship of a purely mortal recreation.

Martyred and demeaned,

following the form of furtive streetward kisses, burning toward the
dawn rubbing raw the skins.

By our englysshes shall we know them and hear such forms of farce.

These are Anglo-Saxons.

Thus is born from clean social monkeys:

suborning, usury, prevarication, and evil spoofèd and satired love;
gripping nails and spears they hurl themselves east or west, raindrops
and bullets reciprocating fog, and forging the unity of our purpose:
they sang:

    "here are we now because we are here now."

Thus golden smoke fell from splintered trees,

the shames unshrouded,

and now it's Corporal Rogers

who's turned into a slurry.

When mortars burst 'pon unpacked graves, the undifferentiated
limbs and skins and organs and heads
sailed high in clouds then liquefied,
drifted and formed a delicate mist through the sunlight and felled
pink rain on all.

Liceshit ratshit and the foetid smell of decaying bodies; they were
one indistinguishable harkening the other, springing onto being and
waiting;

noise chattered the marriage of the louse-combing fire in the nostrils
of flesh, bloated, seeping, dripping rivulets toward the trenches' gain.

Freedom of will and harmony under the splint wrappings oozed the
        memory of leg bits and legs broadcast,
the tense of grinding wretchedness,

gristle and brain and black blood for the sparrows they pooled,
millponds befogged with mists of Avalon and Dunwedin, born anew
another blank cloud of wistful pink,

such strange new forms of men are woven, warriors for some new
heaven of unceasing spite, breads and puddings bowed before the wit
and woe, the lowlands muck and drained, pocked, stippled, rains to
befoul again, thundershowers gathering new souls.
Meat rotting, a fog on London streets curls curbs and cruxes, the flesh
of lads burns itself in molten bubbles of decay, a chemistry of murder
for murder's recipe;

left behind the shreds and derma, the strange waters, oils and grease,
fats aboiling: nutrients;

while torso and its last links are hauled away in thoughtless haste.
    Dark rain in a treeless forest, hearts pled choral for escarpment,
        hillock, dune, or sea-sward, and even fantasies trudge,
slinking in the alleyway, mossy in the hold arocking, scurvied and

abandoned, imperiled, cast away,

marooned on shoals,

forsaken, illiterate, paralyzed—anywhere but here.

They dreamed of home, which consisted of a bed and the dinner table. In those homes only ghosts lived: sister, mother, father: none more real than Morgan le Fey.

The carpenters of duckboards,
the jeweler's assistant, the parson;

duckboards crafted and tendered, and appears the iceman, freshened the cores, cometh the bereavement, trains of deficit, achieving fresh game,

as rabbits rounded for slaughter, coming through raking fire, hopping through slaughter, strafes and enfilade; all by duckboard reposition,

mobilize, agitate for surcease.

Gas and rats,

frost rimes

(From fifty yards a different bacon scent, Fritz' fashion of frying meat.)

Babylon, on the bridgèd valley gander gorge,

on brave brother keen and dear.

Hilly fields and creeks the vision;

grain and chickens, trout,

mine leavened eyes, mine warm wet hands held out to touch, then to hold, then to clutch dear to chest, vanished as a mist.

Winds and breezes rousèd dark 'pon chopped terrain, boding 'biding ghosts seeking warm and fleshy hearts

    to prevail upon the consciousness of memory.
Circuses of spinning bleats and bores,

hailing one another by thrashers and juice;

javelins and sabers and swords and spikes,

daggers and bayonets,

all fend attachments are their motley sundry famished memories, "I clasp your hand!"

The men dug caves in the walls of trenches,

and therein crawled for the thrill of being simply horizontal.

The mind therein reached was delirious leaden slumbering.

Their concentration was upon finding a position in which the chafes did not ulcerate

fleas would drown

and rats could not chew their wet skin.

A soldier did not suppose that

above the trench

civilization had reached the zenith of its

lust for murder,

and its zeal for self-destruction.

A million killed? Two million?

We would not do this to dogs.

Airman farmer fallen here to lay upon their sodden boots, never so
marked as by the touch upon his brow, the sweet shadow of surcease
and demise.
Nothing so bitter as the grey, or so beaten as compressèd browns; the
men the boys smelled the frost in the deepest muds of vainglory.

Blood unrushed, quit to stations, pooling in the veins and curdling in
their arteries, cometh a tighter crouch, acurl as within a shroud.
    These are not grail knights.

Briffault's beakers, basins, bottles stranded on tin shelves erected; the
surgery's double-tented stage;

vaning sacraments,

recitatifs whispered,

preparations, bare bitter moments after darkened sunrise.

He would be planing blood and hands and fingers trough, his boots
molding the clay for still,

ties and ropes he would be yanking,

stanching blurt rivers of blood bile and breath; the earth was rolling
for the artillery,

sweat was the pain best he knew,

'til silence lay a fog upon his ken,

    and then he crippled stillness and dipped his hands into the gaping
        souls and bodies of men and boys rent by mad conceits.

Here everyman hath longing for the end,

the pale green light of the sky, lost,

here everyman stands free from forgetting,

for in a hundred years they will all be gone.

Cathars this way came, in truth and fiendish mobs, to poison wells and bitter creeks;

Crusaders camped and rested, basked in sun.

Brabant Bruges, Roman legions;

these lands learn their ways from Paris and Berlin, and execrate the passage.

On this ridge tenth-century soldiers gathered for slaughter, and eras 'fore that saw monkey-men hack and club red the creeks.

Thus for long hours.

Thus for days beyond days, and in this way three seasons stood upon our brothers' back, of thirst and drowning sobs.

Anchored long in evil's cove,

the breach doth thicken,

doth bind the weak and strong together as one.

My mind is for nausea bred,
hands for digging holes and holes,
the muckmire ocean cruise of shame,
and lists and lists of pollèd names.
My resolution is ignoble cowardice,
to license such knaves as these
to brevet stamps of fault upon my face,

and all I ever was to be,
disgraced among women,
a rotted fruit aground,
hallowed forever and forevermore
a dreamless wretch of shit,
feeble, quarter-hearted, and O! Most foul.

White billows to the rear

copses' foodmen, nurseangels, bookish porters and narrow-shouldered shrouders, the squadron of embalmers' assistants,

buriers, diggers;

horse-drawn wagons slow ahaul beamed and breached the earthwaves back.

Half a portion of a dream, perhaps,

in a small room,

behind the closed door,

reading by a candle lit

by candle lamp,

then closing the book,

and musing,

or perhaps just a feint towards musing.

In such a way after dawn, a cold rain fell on frost that rimed the mud, falling softly as melody.

The gutters of bombshells resembled nothing so much as graves. During Passchendaele distractions paled and then failed altogether to exist.

Death and dying eunuched, achievèd sleep paled death to mud, to
rats, to lice, to affliction, to despair,

to gas and denigrate the air;

committing upon the trenches denigration, blanketing men with tarps
and dynamite's ash, rent faces twisted full round,

stags abash,

the shark's teeth rasping saw;

wickedness found no way out,

and stayed within, to long reside.

Lucy hadn't time (running for knives) to clear the piles of foetid wet
bandages, which toppled over, and to the floor.

Mud caked on tunics before the body was made naked and washed.

Arterial injection; gullies of fluid,

late of the mind, forming the shapes of memory and imagination, a
view of hedge, bedroom ceiling, and perfumed neck.

Behind the lines, the scrap of bushes, trees and weeds near the rut,
and there were stored squadrons of drums of embalming emulsion.

Behind the lines and trenches, dry tarpaulins atop wet hay

and men slept on wet tarps atop drums of embalming fluid at the
woods formed the only 'scape from the mud,

and so there men reposed, unministered at last; many slept, some like
dogs, some like the dead, out of time.

Their minds were sleeping dogs and meditating monks,

at Passchendaele, near Ypres,

on Belgian soil decadent Europe prevails,

and decent Europe dies.

Morning light brought to shape again

the shadows of the observation balloons,

and if there were a far flat crest of brighter sunlight distant in the east,
it might drip only into the heart which remembered each morning
as bread and coffee and the concussive blow of the very first mortar,
banks showed some movement of congealing,

then sweeps of rains across the seas of mud to layer on cloth and
leathers the familiar skin of despond,

the form of gossamer malevolence,

the murders that were hosed in the showers' antechamber of the
theatre of scalpels, where boys troweled hardened blood into barrows
and hauled them to the dark slit

that had lately been a quiet brook

with now no memory

of ever being green and blue.

   You shall know them by their failure of imagination, by their
platitudes; you shall know them by their digressions; and their
contrivances. This plain of death is not a tale, and cannot be
paraphrased.

The study of their minds reveals the chalice,

(the grail was but a shallow dish).

How is love made in Bristol, Essex, Liverpool, Manchester; Halifax,
Winnipeg; displays the heartless mourn of complicit surrender; once
one recovers,

>   but it is the second black trap that turns the mind forever toward
>   angry despair and desperate anger;

you shall know them as they dip their fingers in the coffee; in this way
they can be identified:

fresh from the barn,

clipped from the breakfast table,

rhyming with their ancientmost urges is the call to stretcher, call to pit,

lying in a grave,

cousins rhyme,

Heidelberg and Oxford rhyme,

pickled in brine not for cause but for half-rhyme; by their obsequy
broad panorama kneels the crush of multitudes viewed against sky and
line of horizon;

they shall be known by their humorless submission to the heaving of
the mudfields sliding into shellholes' murk: you shall know them by
the mad ones carried to the copses, loaded onto vehicles,

and excused to barns behind the lines.

Wide-eyed shrunken pips sheeted packed and one waits for breath to
animate the memories or to do so once more never again.

Soaked hemorrhage-heavy, pitched,

boys rutting barrow rearward

along pigeons toward the massive iron quarry,

where conflagration offers different clouds.

Lethargy will fall on all nations, if this war ends.

The freshwater lakes are spoiled with patrician bile.

Men and mankind will look for safety, as always after war they do.
And find nothing but their emaciated and feckless souls, wills, minds,
hearts.

Martin stood over the grey wet litter

and the fragments of his pit companion.

Jim was now gruel,

and Martin was come to some cold comfort peace knowing that this
too was the harmony of the world.

In No Man's Land, a piece of shrapnel half-disembowels a man, and
severs a leg. He lives, not rescued by stretcher bearers for three days,
lying in mud, as a freezing rain falls. He will not die. His calls for help
are unanswered by men in the trench fifty feet away. He will not
perish; his mind—ventures in the horrible present and in memory.
Phosgene gas, from one side or another, stings his mouth and nose
and throat, and then his lungs hemorrhage, turn to red slush, and
what is left of his mortal body and heavenly consciousness, know the
ugliest pain and transport that has ever been described.

By the thousands, the wounded

in No Man's Land lay in agony, calling songs of excruciation.

And from those men hidden

in the trenches?

No response.

> No general ever
> with his own eyes
>
> surveyed the front
> at Passchendaele.

The soldiers had not known death had undone so many.

From wild forests came, and of routine prayer,

birthed in Belgium the true hearts of blood,

vanquished and christened, baptized in the fellowship of fellows speaking, a natter and a gossip,

but boys we are,

and the best of it is rations,

the best of it is rum.

Shrouded and unspoken, the mastery of Leave.

The laid-on fog, the gas, the coverlet of being here now, the school we are, of fingerlings,

the hail farewells.

Wafting o'er Teuton song, they doubtless clutch and wait as we, it's only officers and kings

who boil and break and flense and choke us,

only they who torture.

This terrestrial sea, for all men waves,

and breaks on beaches white and black.

Marty took the cup in his open hand,

and walked to Jack and David, Owen, Lester;

mere chappies

dining in the church-like quiet of the Breakfast Room at the Meurice Hotel in Paris, learning pace and timing,

their nerves and bones studying dying-time.

A quartet of English-speaking fiddles,

    harmonizing their voices softly at twilight
    under lowering clouds of sorrowed doom,
as destinies they watched and heard snuffed by thunder, and turned to blackening curd.

Half a breath pause, some vision at the edges of a dreamscaped stage, a bit known and sensed London griefed,
and ever committed to strange and thickened heart.

And soft the tune picked up again, to lay on those about to fish in pools, with ethered-breath,

the doomed and dead,

carpeting the pocked lands.

The replenishment of a thousand broken platoons is a scavenging through the forests weak,

time-indefinite is a forward-looking memory wasted, desiccated, this is like nothing that has come before, resembles no walking into a wet dark alley,

nor streets that curl between and around muted, silent buildings, boys
shredded arm leg arm ear leg three fingers, and the surgeons step into
the proscenium of demise, washed for the most part too,

of every bit but the dark habits of extrusion and excision, boring for
steel toy parts, rusty nails, spoons, shrapnel balls in the seas of
amputation.

Half-boys carry boy corpses.

The platoons chose one mudhole over another, and lay each fagot
across the arching plane of drippings skyward, scanning only the
essence of form across a way of teasel hedges, cakes of clay,

where disruptions of the form would suggest the source of the track to
stillness ("heaven") or the balls of eye filled with attention and habit to
kill.

In the time of Mordred and queer indefinite ring the boys spoke
together among themselves in pairs or threes according to their social
limitations,

though if there were no bombs of blood flung about boredom
remuddled the pairings and threes according to indifference,
proximity or the deepest tides of attraction and the mingling of
unspoken rhythms.

In truth the death screams descended from the dark soul of man to
a whimper, as within the chest the gorge of spirit breath and blood
tapped a breastbone against the high thin rib,

    reading the surgeons' nod,
    (cats reading doomed mice)
Britain's kings and ministers faultless in exquisite indifference dined,
chauffeurs in the rain awaited brothers' return from the sleep of
conscience in Flanders.

And at the very worst those personifications of evil stratagems born of envy, desire, vanity, and aspirations whose home of heaven is the long table of place settings, achieve the grandeur only of rumor-born winds and lies.

Stretcher-bearers gird themselves with truth,

that life and surcease were always in their every step and breath.

A half-light was dusk or dawn, and sleep was brown storm.

Lacing a general pattern on which to locate either time or the familiarity of such rooms of grieving.

Briffault's recollection caught currents in the canals, lying back on a barge, holding the vision of a recognized bridge, dock, wagons of ashes and bones bound for pits blown with dynamite by the sons of the near others;

and as it would,

the strip of that would sometimes be called the consciousness of Briffault, obeyed the freshets and the surges of change in and on the plain of water, with apparitions and revelations prophesying a thousand ovens.

A thousand ovens will be, comparatively,

a sky-slashing swooping eagle of efficiency,

meticulously sterile, gleaming flashes a lighting strike, as against which the packing into bags the shredded parts of fishermen from Manitoba, and including without prejudice clots of mud doubtless stirred in with the blood of fishermen from Nova Scotia,

farmers near Stuttgart,

and plainsmen from the far west of Ontario,

packed in shroud-canvases like cakes,

> then hied to the theatre of those waste men
> who might have found themselves assuming the responsibility of
> modest preparation of corpses bodies boys for 'fields' nearby,

with embalming fluid from the barrels on which three gloomed suns
ago had lain the fishermen in repose never quite achieving absence.

The flatbreads too had worms.

For we are wrangling beeves and netting oars,

the slang of daytime's prettier whores,

the meads and ales and beers and pours,

do slake our pity and our gores;

our mouths crave the greased swift sword,

the grime of graveled blood we wore,

we leapt in trenches minding lore,

that death crept near our centered core.

The mad signs are vain and broken.

Thus splits the poison gasses with shards shirring razor wire,

mire and mud,
bags of sand and bags of pink,

particles of nails, singeing the gasses,

the puffs of smoke: eyes on mud, open and still, shapen twisted odd
and wheezing,

and lost to the next in line to so die,

eyes on mud,

open, and still.

> Riven souls cleft twice told, bloods and saps mingled mild, sour and
> rich,
> yet warm, yet warm,
> pooling in chemical mystery and magical soil, a sunflower grows
> embracing clouds and rains, and cooked through in chemist's rods,
> a lard of use is mustered lye,
> and vanes of torrent wind and light
> pouring parts of boys amuck in Flanders.

Now the grass is green and lush,

and rats within the cells unshroud the tracks of future tenses.

'Cross Ypres 'virons a perfect distribution of shattered bones, a
harmony a chorus,

an anthem of forgiveness, the solitude of sleep.

> . . . and far to the west
> in the generals' chateaux,
> the wines were a disgrace!

The wheelwright, the butcher's mate, the orewright, the coalwright,
the boatwright's helper,

his bulk of body falling as all deadweights do,

toward the core of earth massed with iron,

thereby removing the brainpan and its dressings
a fractioned moment (blurred in time)

it had before engaged,

as the lead the bullet the slug the shot glided through, thus sparing (for the moment, for a week's time), the clothier, the cook, the mantled don,

the stumpèd bittersman abar,

and the father of Jim Ted Charlie Joe

who might wake from an ignorant snoozing atrain across Belgium bound for icefields of a dying of another color, another sort,

a different blush and hue.

They had not known death had undone so many.

A marling hook, a rusted spike aloft,

brandished threats for skyward: nothing.

How ached the hollow stares cast over Vlaanderen fields, rods of faces, leagues of worms and rats,

papers in the muddy brook,

> and a word is spoken,
> Briffault speaks half-aloud,
> fogged backwards and downwards folded curled, and lost with skin,
> lost with eyes, lost with blood-will-tell,
> blood to sing and chant and wail,

how ached the fevers and the dreams,

as Martin called out a hail of supplication,

and knew not dawn from blackest nighttime clots of clay leavened with the stab, the rich red draught of breath and breathing.

Broken souls in the wrappings screamed, bloods rushed to lakes,
made a mixture rich and gristled, streaked with bile and renal paste,
then baked by lightning rain and storm (some afterthought of
Judas born), a modern spirit swells and mashes down the dream of
picnics, cruelly stacks the boys like logs,
bomb-sawed,
swaddled in briny kerosene,
left to brighten and enrich the soils of Passchendaele, a
long-forgotten stagecraft of primal hells and ever-unpaid debts.

This narcissistic, futile fancy

writ cross flatlands reaching towards the sea,

desert, jungle, woodland, steppe and Transvaal, forest, scapeful cities
of the plain, had not thought but to look up and see the arrows
seeking flesh, had not thought to lay Willie on the tables,

or swill his blood from glass bowls.

Threw they spears and hammers, bolts and axes, swords and daggers,
mace and cannon,

lance and pike; pikestaffs, spears, arrows.

Throats burst as fountains:

this was the sport of eastern frontmen and western frontmen; who had
milked cows,

and carpentered bridges,

and bartered grapes,

and who had simply mined other ores.

Rosebushes planted like cemetery crosses in a grove or hillside pierced
the ground; stay fast the dug-men, hold close the walls,

fling the dagger,
keep your own, sump of Manchester, cess of London.

Ripped to pieces by artillery,

shredded like the lamb; mown from grass to chest, pierced by bullets,
sprayed to arching mist gristle red and stringy, by mortar called home
directly true and callous, in dawnlight Jack and John,

    non-existence to a million dreams.
    This shower of mist is pink and red and dermal.

Fetishes and talismen, amulets, and photographs were assembled in
bags for sure return or were lost to graves and mud, or to
conflagration.

Casualties displayed themselves as outrageous spectacle: faces burned
off, feet and hands,

all the mash of abandon and pity;

mad slashes through the trunk, scooping gouges scattered cuts.

He had waited every minute for the moment,

and when the moment came, he was unaware of time.

Some slime had fastened onto Martin's thigh, and his boot was drying
cold within, Rob is asking for . . . he didn't hear couldn't make it out.

Without surcease, ever standing hard by the holes, palm on the wall,
ever starved for attestation,

clamoring for testimony,

even a word of grace,

the true grains fired and panned for fest,

envisioning a dance

the lessening shore and the dimming sun betrothed.

> Riven souls in the bandages cried,
> torrents of mud slurry and bloods coursed as they would, forgiven
> their flooding of the deltas,
> merged as by an alchemist's false formula.
> Bereft new oversouls dark in the buttered wounds wept, unmercied
> 'pon the scarrèd lands of Flanders rent and fired with scabrous
> tears,
> and men were dried only in the rains' feeble counterpane itself.

> *She asked me was I going to Araby*

Cross the grasslands, narrow near the swamps,

casting steels and irons past,

slender crosses sink in the despond,

city boys and farm lads,

one great awful wave of grain leveled trussed and set afire, like rags and
carcass trunks, like muted horns grieving and blazed.

The prospect of the grasslands trampled raw,

and flows of rivulets apour,

the land of planters torn from grace,

the hovel of the cheapest whore.

Glimmered the fog's frost,

a cloud of iron, canvas, wool, the thousand boys cut, their bitterest
offending wounds of hands crushed and ripped, vagabond sentiments
of loss and absence harked, sung as one chorus mighty and forlorn,

nothing is left of the will of remembrance,

nothing blessèd from Aurignacian caves

peeks pink from youth fresh,

and yet ye shall know them by their blooded guts and ghost, their
phantoms kind and meek,

and by their sweet flesh enriching

the broken soil of broken Belgium.

It seems it must have happened

but a spark of time ago:

you

hear the explosion. Marty is riven.

TWO

But had a lad not been rendered runny,
and had he hied the route of despairing supplication, in a whiter place
would he dwell a while,

where the water was warm, and the fragrance was iodine-salt and
morphine.

Warfare surgery is practiced here, perfected and failed.

Loins opened before Briffault like blooming dahlias, the Empire's
roses from Auckland and Adelaide,
giant bright green thistles from Saskatchewan.

From départements of France.

From counties in England.

From freshwater lakes, and prairies.

Hence: dressings, beakers, trepans, cordage.

Hour after hour, scalpels and saws.

Drums for legs and arms, buckets for fingers.

For endless digging, burrowing in the half-fed, the forgotten and the well-armed, though never quite to situate the transcendental soul, shaped like a cloud, or a crust of bread,

   or otherwise shaped.

But there was other evidence found in organ stews: suborning, dominion, ethnic cleansing, derogation, superciliousness, conceit, chauvinism, bigotry, fanatical intolerance, murder, stupidity, psychosis, and England's implacable constipation and hegemonic, stingy, and ossified resolve of costive ineffectuality.

   The etherized hide nothing.
   Here maiming is perfected: amputation is improved.
   We are for gangrene, scalding, suffocation, asphyxia, and the
   disarray of nerves.
   Foul wounds, blood befouled.

These organ meats are rearranged by queer toffs, repudiating the Moorish renaissance;

these sloshes sluices, bloods and waters funneled into buckets fine; plagues and pestilential vogues and rumors,

   fuel the ripped souls and minds;
alcohol rains the rigging, squashing every embryo in kind; blast royal betrayal, blast treacherous House of Lords, sylvan rural planters despoiled the crops, by usury pined.

These organbags threshed and minced,

these Englisher boys shredded, ripped

quartered as by mad stallions,

and melted, burned, sizzled, boiled and fried.

The loam of earthsoil is leavened with skin.

The air was gassed by black knights with the stench of a towering and howling mendacity.

The scale in which this tableau is measured is named by all observers broad! Accreted in the rural Belgian treasury, as stalks of golden wheat, then ravaged and lost by wicked puerile manliness, in fires of half-felt rage, were the innumerable lives of those all who once-were-children.

Moorish children, Moroccans, Mauritaneans,

and the black Spanish who had never known anything but peace; "AMITIE," quoth gold ribbons and silver bands, one delicate necklace.

A sweet savor of remembrance,

the aroma of bread baking in kitchens darling and beloved, to a lark of precious song;

adventuring by bicycle across the valleys to Iola's purple gorge, vineyards and horticulture blooming the yields of fare; itinerant scholars' poems gathered;

the serving girl was dazzling, her breasts ungathered, as she carried to Briffault's table a beer.

His reflection piercèd back in epochs, stranding braids of seaweed curled, memora cresting on no far shore, simply to drift in doldrums dear, and gradually bracket scenes and smells, dinner warm in a rough hotel,

Laura wringing pulp from rind, a tortoise shell embraced the mind.

Sunray-spangled countenance, so close as ever may we get to angels,
it seemed to be a dream in which she took my hand and seaward
strolled, the glimmering shine of stardust lit;

remembrances in bright profusion hued the sense of crazed allusion,
yet of kindness peace and liberty.

Dawn approached, bedewed the sunflower, plaits and tresses crowned,
as mist obscures the valley, as mist rebukes the dawn.

Fainting in the *jouissance* merry, hearts to mingle with a faerie.

    This nymph sundered
    knows nothing of dying for all the death she has served whole, and
does not suppose herself clinging to a straw as black storms gather and
strange winds rage, his precipice of sainthood peeked beneath this leaf
of cotton succulent and sopping,
    the wolves of war engorged with might,
    and then is fallen darkness fallen full.

She crossed the patio looking as usual like a million dollars, lacking
parceled glamour and allure, yet vivid, brilliant, a light of English
spake, the green light of "slumbereth now 'til Venus." So Briffault
dreamed his waking reverie.

Flowers fall from clouds, petalling the path and grass, the skin of roses
and the hands of lilies,

and there we lay in anisette, fennel and jasmine, the wines they bore,
and absinthe, vanilla cakes, drunk mad to skies and nestled in the
silent bower, a nest for love, remembrance, alone and safe,

sheltered in their eyes entwining mirrors upon mirrors.

The troubadour songs came up from Spain,

> in which crucible of contested courts of love black gentlemen pled
> > to sing blackbirds and blooms,

the merry delights of unsophisticated gathering, drinking, singing, and
joys unnamed.

Night for days, festal feast of visions, bread and wine, a russet claret,
the croissant crescent, barged across the Mediterranean Sea.

Now the season leans to dimming, and the leaves escape to earth; the
slanted sun steals light from sported vespers, gloom hushes birdsong,
song and whistles,

we can but rest, we can but convalesce,

> we can but wake to bullets raining.
> We muse in gape and stupor. More rain. More mud.

Half-waking, brute cannon threw damp shadows dark upon the men,
to hide the sun behind the rains;

and sheltered lee from misery, such gales and storms depraved, against
the gentility of the natural man exposed to butchered life.

Such breezes bore the trace of a cigarette, and we lay amid the
hawthorns, embraced by clouds and love itself,

spread 'pon the soft grasses and spongy reeds.

Heavy our hearts with leavetaking, laden our dreams with dread, the
rushing bloods of ardor, the fervid tears of weeping shed; hath gone
nowhere but t' having gone,

a wisp of perfume, detected after we arrive,

the warm gossip of humankind,

a little flame of soul has lately flickered here.

Now the night grows darker

to murks of lightless pall,

a fade of hope and the breath of sighing;

weak clouds cross the moon to shelter and despoil such privacy as we
might steal from libelers' force,

    it is as if we remain all to bed, and undisturbed call sprites and imps
        of kindest brand, to nestle with us twined.
Perch astream share and fry their flame of life,

and roast 'tween toasts of currents blue and pure and sweet and
by-your-lips so blessed,

your blood blended chirps from branches benign, which bade us stand
'gainst villains,

who'd violate the carriage crimson heading back to Montparnasse.

Fools are wrought by grim psychosis;

grassland lowland pampas green,

with sparkling brooks slowly angling,

calm bouquets for contemplation.

Restless the eyes of the heart, quakes the memory of other lands.

Some conveyance brought us here, magical and sinister, and now
dreams like mists rise from meadow,

    and freshet back to homes our softened views.
    Sharing biscuits and tea,
    conspiring with comrades 'gainst the chill, the bonds of voices

exchanged in unreserved truth.

Exposed to consider whatever repair might be massed, whatever effects
might be rendered,

> or what conjuring might be committed upon the spill and slosh of
>   bowels and blood and general organ saps
the surgeon saw shamed madness,

the manifest condescension of the mongering British, who would
eliminate a generation in the name of naming so.

A Rouen maître d'hôtel arrived on canvas and pole, hauled by
fifteen-year-old boys,

> (or were they crickets?
>   or were they tulip stalks?).
His blood was chaste, and on the hands and face it spurted kisses,
these Andalusians, these Basques; these Provençal colporteurs, deers
and ducks, these Berliners, those from Bonn,

monkeys, kittens, cockatoo,

a treasured zoo,

these learnèd souls of temperance and trick-chieved loyalty.

Poor medicine for seraphs; pallid surgery for such true blood.

Drawn out upon the twilight, tears of sheerest kindness.

Hard rearranged in the bag, useful units of life, and in the flesh still
beat the heart,

though seams were pricked and tunnels severed, and the pouches
spilled sauces among one another; let us stand still half a moment
pretending with these swaddling nurses

that all is quiet all is calm,
pretend that smothering sentiments of beatitudes have like a
counterpane warmed us all.

These men are kittens.
The tiny heart beats;
then ceases to beat.

Afterwards: Briffault reflected that the blown-out body of Martin
showed the bread he'd lately taken,

and the scent of the apportioned

rum provided before the charge.

A pinker blood than common here, a tapeworm, and a tiny spleen.

Slashes, abrasions, scene obscene.

His hair was blond as legend's blond,

his hands were scratched and raw, and strong;

his face beatific.

Smiling still, and in the corner of an eye, unmistakably a twinkle,
Surely this, the spark of his nirvana.

But what be this talk of bread (quoth Reggazoni, Malatesta) when
seabirds unconcealed paint the sky with uneaseful smiles, and free the
flowers of imagined reverie?

The British Expeditionary Forces became masters of a simpler and a
softer bread; ten-pound loaves had proved too rude.

The art of baking bread in the field, behind the lines some, grilled
night and day and night, stood against the sewage not at all, nor
contravened the smoking fleshes, the marrow fires, hair smoldering

and dissolved.

The breads hardened and crusted to perfection, and though torn off loaves by anxious nerves,

it felt still warm, for such delectable kissing it always seemed to be.

Yet there it lay, ungraced, entrapped in trencher's cuppèd gut within: bound for a narrow grave, pickled and limed,

  his name writ again and again in paperwork.

Perfectly and 'til the end of time

sucked by gluttonous writs of Elizabeth First,

eternal blame for brute stanching the many dawns of scholarship peace and love; for making sea war on the Iberians;

for betraying the natured people of North America, and for eviscerating the kingdoms of the east,

poisoning the water,

burning the ricecrops,

scorning the peasants

and deriding the holy men.

Every thirtieth litter carried into the English dressing station bore an Angle or a Saxon of Germanic tongue,

whose slash or scald, whose skin aboil or poached or fried, for madness only mirrored boys from offshore isles, their red wet hacks and burning flesh and tender wits and dreams

  shattered and defiled.
The scent of favored rations on the tunic or lips varies some, but the

bushels' and the buckets' pride would boost the clover and the poppy, though staff would not merry up this truth

to complex diction and troubled rhyme;

the meter remained as pure as Latin, a hundred after hundred passeth through, from dark trench wet and morbid on

> to trains to Channel ports,
> or more quickly to filled and nearby pits.

As certain, Hrothgar wipeth rough the king's table, dumpèd vanquished sundered sons, he beginneth his rummage, plucking and thumbing the hacking gape,

and soon discover split or rent,

the riven pot of organ meat,

the gushing rush of fluids gained.

In the manner trained, Briffault spoke the idiom of stiff medicines, cloaked in the piffled English-speaking voice,

> and followed forms and orders made;
> but the polymath was beset by guides,
the very competence of nurses,

and this one from Leeds, Lucy,

her courage and her pity clear,

reminded him of Beatrice,

and his whole heart and literature were changed, altered to the warm light of Moorish glowing reading, as Alighieri shit on popes and dismal leashmen.

His transcendent spirits flocked home to the brown skin of one lass,

and there remained, and there captured the ringing calls to peace of
Alla ben Bazir, and the blood brain breath of the warm supple acumen
of *il miglior fabbro*.

My heart! How they scurry, steaming prows of Cathay, commerce prigs
and dhows plying grain and silk, trades for lucre, chess of retribution;
how the nurses scurry mid the groaned or stilled beds, when some
flied kerosene clouds cross bandages bereft and burning; how masks
are affixèd, how men are hustled under tents anew, and scrounging
for breath mid the dumps and cellars of foetid-timbered hovel; how
they dash and scamper, young girls from Leeds and London, wherefore
thou art lost to cape pulled over sweethearts, urgent to hide the lover
from the scornful looks of the most vile slanderers.

Imperial roses, royal houses rot, chamberlains imagine heads apike, to
spark blood fear in tindered kindling children.

Bestoweth arch the monkeys' love,

and bury plain the monkeyed men.

Filled a'gunnel, gauze and cotton,

beakered morphine, opium drums.

Morning hearthman, gathering spouses,

before the remains' homecoming,

the undifferentiated soul,

and aboard a flatknife, allocated evenly aplate the side, those soon
whose hands would soak in soap and spattering bloods merged in
simmering pails.

Woman glowing golden, crowned in glory's dawning hues of rose and
flaxen dale, a thumb and finger of crumbs, kiss Lucy's lips;

and sips the tea the instant bomb splits the air
and this warrior's solid stainless stalk of trunk.

Souls liveth here.

Soon the bad season will be over and with it the gale and the dusk
    and the hoar which now show themselves openly over boughs
void of any leaf; since now no bird sings or chirps there,
love then bids me stir such a song as to be neither second nor third,
but first in sweetening a sour heart.
Over by the impoverishment of wheat and oil, by no other will, nor
leafing of the angel, nor the whippoorwill whose tax is but to sing,
and soften the evening sunlight for placid, sleeping lover.
Love is the key to worth
and to valour it is paramount where all the best fruits are born, if
there's one to pluck them loyally, since none is spoilt by frost or fog,
while it feeds on the good bole:
but if broken by the wicked or treacherous, it withers until a
righteous lover blesses it.

This lass from Leeds, holding hands by night of splintered skins and
savaged bones.

Pools and pans endlessly pouring,

portioning morphine, a last kiss at dawn before the watchman's hark
and hollow call.

The heart mended after a steady travail, to watch the breathbags
drowned, and lost.
To stand corrected in wrong is praise;
and I feel in both my sides that I bring more love, doubtless, than
those who talk and brag, since it makes my heart more feeble:
while she was smirking at me, I would rather have roamed,
penitent, in deserts where no bird has ever nested.

Self so same these boys slaughtered 'neath my hands rebuke me
with their honor and pity.
I swim against the stream of waters tasteless; I swim against the
current raging.

This war is a song concerning which occidental ears await melody
in vain.

In these songs I sleep beside the river tranquil still as stone.

This sleeping waking life, hold close my scenes and forms therein
derived, together zephyrs and gusts shape an arch cross roiling rivers
and spacious seas, the fusing of rackets, the aggregating pot of song's
romance, the philosophy of sociable tribes, oryx and gentleman.

The cheerful men from Twickenham, called boys to trenches pits and
holes.

The captured and the meek refused to show their failure or their fear,
and so they fled toward graves for spite and beast's discomfiture.

Such purity is mine, to scream, for Jack is dripping on my vestments, a
rivulet, a current;

none shall see just this: blasts overarching cowherd's bell.

The plumes arear, black smoke rising:

as in miniature before us and around us so,

puffs of memories vaporating and running off and up to seed the
rainclouds, thence to fall on buckets basins blood and thin potato
soup.

There was ample water, food, no whisper of war arose; the plazas
were citadels of the marrying arts and bread.
Each child a vortex of demand and piercèd frame, learned in

schools, rings of sopping minds 'neath trees and sun swards, and in circles be, apprenticed by masters and peer kins.

In its place we tremble in the latter days,

and roses wither moist and black;

acids foul the brooks and clot the white cascades; the cozy homes of blood are torn and slit.

Men are made eager to hunt and seize,

to make witness of their living by the murder of another's breath.

As here beneath the striving hands the discord plays itself, a killing foul, the knotty plots of Jacquesfather, whose forebears from near Barcelona came,

and 'for that Marrakech;

then boarded ship for Rowan Oake,

whose ire and woe writ large and played out full, pictured these scenes of barren deserts and raw dismemberment.

In the latter days of torture, the final field of hate, men whistled cross the bloodied mires, and pardoned suffered mates.

They seemed to beg Sahara come and blot wet Belgium dry, these kings and princes self-made by diseasèd fevers, a plague of psychosis,

worms mince in the garden of the oblongata.

Within the dugout hovels, tents, and barns,

the ceaseless coming going,

by error and by egocentric laziness,

stretcher-bearers bore men with but three

breaths left,

bestowing shallow time on next,

> whose chance at life ever afterwards befell a girl from Leeds, and
> Briffault, the surgeon,
> whose craft at angling from mad rapids swift trickster fishes, would
> pitch to home or Flandren grave
> a boy the forms called Martin.

His arrival in the unearthly glow of several lamps, with incision already
made,

> sopping endless, sopping done,
as so many men before; part recently removed.

Within this surgery's light Briffault remembered the piazza, and after a
day of exuberance,

Carlotta crossing the way to his table,

looking as usual like a million dollars.

Her form and perfume, abiding, her lips on the delicate glass, she
smoked and smiled and hit multitudes,

far lands of trains at night, he lay the scalpel 'cross his palm, soft on
the fingers, then began to free the organs together congealing, began
to trim a vessel and a sack,

to appraise the ribs new-formed by shattering steel.

> There is no sense in which he lives in pasts.

He has only his puzzlement,

> and the two at the table have only their relation, and their obeisant

and affecting compliance of purest attention.

Gossip-mongers wreck privacy and undo dreams, and pike-stab the peace of those who would but share bread with lover.

This war without reason annuls each hopeful rosy dawn, and blots the distant fires of cooking 'cross the creek.

Explosions christened with bowed hands in prayer, fair bodies blond and reluctant,

each barrage born of indifferent brimstone,

but hellish fire nonetheless,

heave 'cross the matted meadow molten metals of inclemency, ceaseless and indomitable invasion of fair bodies, the human parts whistle like sirens,

whirling and spiraling 'cross the grazing land,

catching breathing skin on boys from East London.

The machinery of this war mows men flat,

and slithering in muddy slimes they do forget why here they came, and which demented snobs brought them forth.

They had been pure, they all had been pure,

before their suborning by the fat and vain and cruel.

Their lives were love affairs, and rhapsodies of afternoon tea or beer.

Together Saxon and Angle played hearty base, a game, 'til monstrous forms of evil came in greed and fear, in the rhetorical dimension.

Spake thus, Raimbaut d'Aurenga.

Standing over the boy—Martin, Canadian Expeditionary Forces—
Briffault murmured, half-aloud:

Als durs, crus, cozens, lauzengiers
Enojos, vilans, mals parliers
Dirai un vers que m'ai pensat;
Que ja d'als no·i aura parlat,
Qu'a pauc lo cor no m'esclata D'aisso
qu'ieu ai vist e proat
De lur malserva barata,

picking out the first visible chunks and flecks of shrapnel, a harvest of
intrusion, this wicked abutment of conceits, this clash of innocents,
the murderous boredom of acculturation

and the customization of perjured souls once benevolent and
sympathetic; the capacity for sympathy treated by steel to a feast
macabre.

To the hard, cruel, scalding slanderers—annoying, vile,
ill-speaking—I will sing a song I have devised;
for it shan't treat any other subject,
for my heart is about to burst because of what I have seen and
experienced of their evil trickery.

Men expire here, quickly gone to death.

Red hearts split and burst, geysers bite back bold 'gainst those who
mock the mud burbling like fat frogs; the grass bows as caissons pass,

white-robed red-crossed Quakers mark the path to the crematories.

Larks in meadows for a moment lay still, abranch, in shadows dark and
unforgiven.

Waves of grains bent to breeze, no more,

for them waves of dying boys have been ignobly swapped.

The tree stripped bare of leaves is charred by thunder and shaken by white flashes; returneth the creeks and brooks to pike,

returneth the warrens to otters and badgers;

here bucolic song betrayed,

as mighty tortures and fierce improvident wastrels and felons growl gainst the bawdies and grim the bowls;

messengers town to town splayed to grease,

young lovers strolling meadow tufts and hillocks espy waltzed evening for loves unmingled,

out of time with the former and the latter scene gross rank and overweening acts 'pon the stage of cradle-tipping malice, Maladicta, murdering broken sage within all men's hearts.

Efficient paths are natured, not from plans, the dead go left and stay dead, the dying go straight,

and those without courage remain in pits and holes aswamped by gore and blood, there to wither in cowardice and unpitied rancor.

These boys and girls never ask why they have come to the unspeakable heart of malevolence and vice.

Such chancrous sores, such pustules flowing,

rivers sourced in the blackest envies.

Skies of cloud and skies of grey,

horizons of emptiness;

snows dress breads with soot.

This Children's Crusade, fishing dry the sea of boys, rendering onto corpses the noble and the dim, once to have come upon this land unbeknownst even to one's own visions, the liberty of culture cleaned and the peace of stories yet unpenned; copse and vista green and rich with soil and water, soft mosses of sleep and bread for the morning feast and gossip.

Hath love a finer dove?

Millions of lives were lost, the study of a few of which revealed the unrealized promise of sculptors and poets and philosophers.

But the letters home which one finds hard by the skin of millions of dying men foretold only lives that would have been mired in decades of boredom and desperation and rancid servility.
Lives ended at twenty would have amounted to nothing but travail and sorrow, sixty years of hardship, abuse and abusing;

and to what we would call "insignificance."

A hundred men made this war. Their disdain understood that perishing soldiers would have awful lives;

that they would die by the millions, once and always "small" men.

Ten men decided that the war would continue; it was fought on a few hundred acres

for the name and pride of nations. So they averred.

We had not known so narrow a field as this

could sweep the choirs of Belgium bare.

The earths, the soils, the grounds of strifeless peasants honor no prince,

but only the streams and ponds which here hold fish of many colors.

He imagined himself aswim awading

in the briefest stare 'pon canvas-poled,

the communion of time and no-time,

the bread and wine of liberation,

and recreated the quiet of the breakfast room of the Meurice Hotel; what kind soft roles here we play,

the music from another room;

plying the snip of the flarèd nostrils, the tides of compounds; the sugars and fats and spices of glands and glands unknown; or the eagle's shriek of pure looping flight,

a roll against the current and a kitestring for the sun.

Keep delinquent betrayers, the defalcation of whores; yet poppies there blossomed,

and sitting at a corner table with coffee and bread and cigarettes, one then might study the philosophers' deliberations sweeping against the ruined people, the squashèd aptitudes of these children,

threading back through centuries of affliction and cringing, booting to the gutters the gathered insight,

leaving no man to saunter hard by Erewhon

    or faint by reckless mad and beautiful dreams deferred.
    This war broke everything
    except the barriers between the social classes.

And then the scene was sickening,

and then the vista reeked,

Briffault bowed his head in shame and reckoning, and turned aside to
Lucy:

"Speak now, and tender, Beatrice nurse of Leeds, to soften Marty's
leaving."

The unleavened soul that depicts Martin's inherent transcendent deity,
(with a trim of storms and a thunderous starry cloud of birds,

unfolding as a supernatural essence, with light), consists of an
aggregated stewpot of gravity,
oscillation,

sunshine,

seawater,

chlorophyll,

and metaphor,
all in the name of clairvoyant love.

Envoi

Yet such submission to befouled authority was necessary to protect the
sacred flame of *jemenfoutisme*

So shall we say

that the only people who achieved a true memory of Passchendaele,
and what it might have been for,

and what it might have made

are the rougher kids who scuffle in the streets,

who roam in packs,

    aimless one place to nowhere.
    (As after the American Civil War, other heart-worn johnnies never
saw the point in anything anymore,
    and gave themselves over to wandering, languishing in exultant
laziness, and sitting on porches, for years and more, in a North Carolina mountain crossroads town called Loafers Glory.)
Electively removed from economics (which caused the War), these
street imps are the "proofs" of shell-shock.
This is a place where nothing is celestial.

These punks will fight in no other man's war.

    These tramps are angels—
    angels of the dharma.

And a girl called Daisy (Daisy Miller, after a fashion),

is wild in the streets,

thieving wine and bread and fags,

orphaned, yet still by such as these freed

from generations of nonfeasance,

treachery, and vanity.

Boulevard waifs gathering from the burned-out stars, in twos or threes
or gangs or mobs.

Unruly loud in neat cafes,

perhaps a few impulsive crimes;

mischief 'gainst the bourgeoisie;

a few bright pitchèd firy bombs;

> and a frantic search for blood
> and kicks.

Scuffling and scamping

in streets and alleys,

shiftless in the pathways,

singing on the terraces,

blending with the shadows

in the less genteel edges

of the otherwise hospitable Paris parks.

Near the Mètro tracks,

young people gather to smoke cigarettes and pot, and gather to harass the weakling bores

to mock the stupefied,

with their freight of promise,

and their sham of hope.

In their every reverie and every dream

they shake off the dead hand of traditional heredity.

> A single word fitteth here:
> Rebellion.

From Passchendaele?

Our single true prize

assumes the form of natural delinquency, by

street urchins, runaways, and waifs.

The world was Modern, for a time, then peaked, then tipped back to sulphur.

In the trenches there were no epigrams or proper nouns, but by January 1919 the pigs had come back out of their offices, in which they lived the whole of their lives,

and reasserted their dominion over the insufficiently brave.

Yet angels in the dooryard bloomed,

and Eden is by forfeit lost

then by transgressive mercy gained,

here, in Paris today,

where the rays of the grand warm sun

come precisely to rest upon these gamine children musically,

by dance,

and by kisses of the very merriest kind.

> Go doest thou,
> and revel only in thy private paradise,
> the 'thou shalt not' is lifted here.
> The soul sings songs
> heard only by its lonely heart.

vi.

TROBAR CLUS

During two years of isolated rustication (lakeside, without running water, 1975 and 1976), I hiked into town and wandered through the stacks of the Wells College Library in Aurora, New York, and by chance looked into a copy of Robert Briffault's *Europa*. It was an event that pointed me in a direction I did not then identify, as I searched—as must we all—for the real and the true. In what might be called a fit, I then read and re-read the two *Europa* books, and have ever since been unable to surely distinguish many of Briffault's prescriptions from my ventrilo-quial notions. At the same time I was reading the entirety of the printed work of all the Provençal troubadours, and *The Ambassadors*, *The Wings of the Dove*, and *The Golden Bowl*. It was Kate Croy, quite specifically, who bridged Briffault and James, and with whom I could colloquize my uncertainties. In the approximate era of this immersion, I would visit the city, and two friends and I would debate our impressions of Kate, over the dinner table and its couple of hours of ice melting in the martinis and cigarettes stubbed in the dessert plates. *The couple shared a drag from one cigarette, locked eyes, then stepped toward oblivion or to the pale postponement of some other oblivion.* I pled Miss Croy's whole absence of malice or design, and consequently learned the topography of the gap between her and Julian Bern. This turned out to be quite exactly the scaling measures of my trepidation, which I had recognized as the vital and absolute difference between the two forms of intentionality, and as the bitter hatred of aphoristic clichés. Combined with self-reliance, that is a modern Emersonianism, and if I could not carry its weight, it did provide me with a keen enough eye to at least usefully spy autonomy and the inherent benevolence of contravention. I regard the dinnertime quarrel of three lovers as a quandary which an understanding of the war would have easily resolved, by means of asking myself if I would have been, in the trenches, brave, or brave enough. I am now unable to believe that I could have comprehended the war without having first understood Henry James and Robert Briffault. Kate and Julian were achieving the same impossible goal.

I am unable to suppose that Harry Crosby's well-planned suicide was not conceived mindful of the wide fields of death he experienced in the ambulance corps, any less than Ravel's *le tombeau de Couperin* could have achieved its spell without the loss of his friends, or cummings' *The Enormous Room* without his 1917 imprisonment. I could not know war without the novels and memoirs that illuminated the forces that allowed the war to exist. History had declared that two platoons were eliminated. A novel invited us to examine twenty four hearts split open by shrapnel and leaking into shitty, bloody mud. And while I had rather a lot of feelings for the Iroquois who lived in the basin at the south end of Cayuga Lake and along its eastern shore in Chonodote (Aurora), these pastoral oriental naturalists, even in their savage repulsion of Sullivan's Expedition, directed by General Washington "to do mischief" to the natives by burning their peach orchards and souls,[9] had not prepared me for the European Golgotha of warfare and its tyrannical method of separating courage from cowardice. The Iroquois were fiercely matrilocal, and their league of federation prefigures, according to some, American democratic constitutionalism. As one in some fashion feels directed by forces before they can be named, I had in fact been exposed to enough of the droll drama of life to have then pointed myself to Passchendaele. But I did not. I jumped on a bus bound for Raleigh, North Carolina, and there immediately came under the influence of E. Paul Campbell (a forester in Mali and Haiti, a teacher of Qi Gong, the sort of person to whom appellations of 'saint' are appended). In

his influence, I bought a bicycle, and discovered locomotion, independence, and the serviceable illusion of feeling guiltless. At 4:00 A.M. I
rode the streets of humid Raleigh, each streetlamp a moon. Years later,
I returned to upstate New York and bicycled everyplace, well-learning
the topography of the Finger Lakes as if I were scouting the hills and
ravines for a subsequent assault. Skaneateles, Cazenovia, Keuka Park,
Canandaigua, Cooperstown, Onondaga Nation Territory, Canadice
Lake. A bluish-green bicycle was the mechanism that removed me from
electronics, hysterics, and representationalism. It had provided me with
my first perfectly apposite scale. And then in an experience familiar to
compulsive readers and obsessive learners, it was beginning to seem to
me that nothing did not strandentwine back to the Great War. But by
that intertextual jollity I was neither perplexed nor dismayed, "and that
has made all the difference." Alain-Fournier wrote in the chapter "An
Apparition" in *Le Grand Meaulnes*:

> I had never before been on a long cycle ride: this was the first.
> But, despite my bad knee, Jasmin had for some time been teaching
> me to ride. And if for an ordinary young man a bicycle is a very enjoy-
> able conveyance, just imagine what it would have seemed to a poor
> boy like myself, who until recently had had to limp along, bathed in
> sweat, after less than four kilometres! Plunging down from the top of
> a hill in the depths of the countryside, discovering the distant road
> ahead like a bird on the wing and watching it open and blossom
> around you, dashing through the village and taking it in with a single
> glance. . . . So far only in dreams had I experienced such delightful,
> airy motion; even climbing the hills I felt full of energy, because, I
> have to admit, it was the road to Meaulnes' place that was flying
> beneath my wheels . . .

It was exotic and gothic, but the redemptive power of the bicycle had
allowed me to find the right tense to imagine myself in the trenches,
by means of Briffault's descriptions, yet also by means of his dissatis-
factions and animuses. We achieve concordance where we may, and in
the junctioning of the bicycle, and certain books, and certain people,
was a synthesis of elective affinities that gave me eyes to see. It was an

integration, the sort of which I had not imagined possible—the nature of which I had always been strenuously suspicious—until I experienced the personal relevance of *souplesse*: the cyclists' metaphor of a naturally-occurring harmonizing of breath, blood, stroke of the pedals, and the symphonic whirr of the perfectly tuned derailleur.

"Night Thoughts of a World War I Medical Officer," an occasional faux-Anglo-Saxon, mock Elizabethan iambic pentameter may suggest a dissonance of subject and manner; but the historical voice, the poetical voice, the voice of enchantment, and the voice of historical reverence were all untenable, having been macerated beyond usefulness in the mills of repetition and prosaica. The lyrics are a vernacular of an unalloyed and underived glossary, but vaguely reminiscent and feigned syntax may be a sure way to remove a language of expectation. The war was pointless murder in its own unique lexicon; it was idiomatic tergiversation; it was the language of lying. (When asked why he had gone to Arabia, Colonel T.E. Lawrence replied that he went there "in order to rescue English Prose from the slough into which it had fallen.") The slate in the Poet's Corner at Westminster Abbey calls forth Wilfred Owen's

> "My subject is War, and the pity of War. The poetry was in the pity."

The undifferentiated calamities of the war created certain obtuse conditions and relations, and the passive voice may best suit the human despair and the abhorrent physical conditions of Passchendaele, with its lacks and obscurities, its constant malice and woe, and its vapid sense of there being nobody in charge. The war demanded the voice of anomie; the object of the war was malevolence, yet it seemed to come without a subject. The voice from the stage, and the perfervid intention of a gaited blank-iambic buffer against a naturalism that might seep into an account of events that must belong outside historiography, journalistic recollection, and sentiment. It is in this same manner that reckless allusions and untethered references afford us a new place from which to consider the scene. Siegfried Sassoon speaks of the "demented language" of the War, and only those wholly enveloped by it can speak the breadth of its syntax and its awful and ambiguous connotations.

The text of "Night Thoughts of a World War I Medical Officer" may favorably come to mind in a theatrical venue, abetted by an actor's gestures, asides, and apostrophizations. There are instances where both semantics and denotation are vaporized. The performative voice might affect an euphonious trilling and vocal larking suggestive of spoof or satire. Madness and comedy commingle. A reader elicits laughs from the swelling swoops of the declamatory and histrionic lyric-singsong. Shakespeare's cadences are the iron core of the English language, and readers may recall that pockets of hillbillies in America and dells of rougher folk in Britain have preserved the actual sounds of his texts. Dotson Rader and Gore Vidal have noted Tennessee Williams' penchant for erupting a loud, rancorous laugh of hilarity at performances of "Streetcar" (at just the moment one character mentions her reliance on persons unknown for supportive benevolence), thereby desecrating for the audience what had been a stilled and sublime theatrical moment. There was a wry mood of irrelevant humor in the trenches; else the place was only hell observed.

The years of the Great War, and those just preceding, and those just following, are commonly associated with the birth of "the Modern," in prose, thought, and the Great Unshackling, with its jazz, salacious dance, sex, alcohol, and its new concept of leisure, all of which implied the corrosion of royalism and inherited authority. But that is a modernity which recurs afresh in each individual, most particularly when hope is lost, and people affirm for themselves that merely prevailing shall be considered the cardinal attribute. The resonance of the war relates to time, but it is a time that is non-chronological, completely dependent on consciousness, and free-floating: men in the trenches and women in the aid tents observed the moment of passage from life to death as a mere flutter. It is axiomatic to note that we are these days drenched in satire, in both its subtler and blunter forms, but a transcendent kind of satire, relating specifically to the First World War has never really materialized. The war had comic aspects (prefiguring the Pythons), but it can never be elevated to irony. In just the same way, the First World War was mediaeval, but the Second World War was historical. Fluctuating and politically-evolving waves of opinion about the Great War washed over the citizens of London and Berlin, but it was those German-speaking peoples with a history of cherished abstracting philosophies who first came to regard the battles of annihilation just *as* annihilation, and not some grand nationalistic enterprise. To contravene the lies of the English newspapers, soldiers returned to Picadilly to exclaim by their mere presence, fantastical monologues of pointless loss. The real reverberation of the war was tapped out by hundreds of one-legged soldiers, their crutches on the street producing a percussive crescendo of truth. A portion of the people of the city were now legless, armless, eyeless, lacking memories, lacking coherence. They were incongruent in the most absolute manner. The post-war years were a kind of participatory folklore by which society's amnesia and refutation exposed the essential pointlessness of the Great War, and men knew that the inherited world of manners, relationships, and authority they took into the war had not come out quite intact. Nothing was assured, and whether or not they ever expressed it, a seed of anarchy dwelled within them all. Modernism declared that our minds are not beholden to time. To the degree that we, as century-later readers have faith in the truth of our empathy, we may notice that we too are making connections that seem illogical and arbitrary. Disparate sensibilities may suddenly rhyme; memories branch and reconnect; time becomes place, and locale becomes duration, aural assaults become touch, and it may become quite evident that the last vestige of Oedipal exploration is death itself; as so it was for millions.

Briffault's Passchendaele marries primary and secondary sources to conjecture what might have passed through the sublimely-educated mind of a humanist living through the violent apotheosis of cultural degeneracy. His own attempt to stanch the tide of corruption was simply to salvage the lives of countless wounded young men. I had found that I was disgusted with people who exhibit the familiar habit of studying the war without writing about or taking it personally. We do not merely empathize with those persons eliminated by the war, and we do not simply remember them: if we do not understand the way in which we have been changed, and do not feel the contemporary behavioral contradictions of the war, then we should be regarded as cowards.

Such lines as these can make no particular assertion other than the inadvertent about the more scrupulous forms of historical representation, and they contravene most if not all of the standard scaffolding-joints of aesthetic presentation. They mean to keep alive the flame—in any of its forms—of the *musée sans murs*, and cultural anthropology textbook, and Beckett's *I Can't Go On/I'll Go On*, that was Passchendaele and the other battles of sacrifice and attrition.

In April of 2012 Kathleen and Rick Hynes-Bouska made materially possible my expedition to Germany, France, and Flanders, for the examination and contemplation of the countryside and reminiscent traces of the sites of Third Ypres, Passchendaele. Kathy and Rick and I walked around the village now called Passendale: the place is exceptionally clean, orderly, and shows no trace whatsoever of its medieval era, as nothing remains built before 1918. The little lake at Zonnebeke was ringed with competitive fishermen, each angler perfectly silent, and I thought of the miners who a few yards away, ninety-five years before, had whispered among themselves as they planted explosives meant to kill hundreds.

The Passchendaele Museum is located in Zonnebeke; we are there the day before the celebration of Vimy Ridge, where it is always stated, truly, Canada's national identity was "forged." A hundred Canadian high school students have come to Belgium to attend the ceremonies; visiting with them, Kathy, from North Bay, Ontario, weeps freely for her kin who perished. At that moment, for her, the war was ongoing. Driving around Flanders, it is impossible not to notice the tiny cemeteries, German and British, tucked behind hedges, or nudging up against farmers' fields. The landscape in no way resembles the aerial photographs taken during the war, when the ground was uniformly pocked with shell holes. Then there were no trees with leaves, and even the courses of the creeks were distorted. When we passed through the Menin Gate at Ieper (Ypres), the central square and the renovated Cloth Hall flared with social activity: tourists, jugglers, bands, beer-trolleys, and marketeers. Buses unloaded Belgian schoolchildren for their spring history rounds. In this city they celebrate Kaatenstoet, commemorating the ratting cats thrown from the top of the Cloth Hall in medieval times. We are an hour from Dunkerque; Bruxelles is not far, but that is a place of another time for René Magritte and Jacques Brel. In the summer, the flower fields are lush, green gardens. A wedding in seventeenth century Vlaanderen costume disturbs our sense of the separate times that we suppose that we are trying to integrate. An old man tried to sell us bits of unearthed metal, putatively century-old combat shards. The Menin Gate Memorial contains the names of fifty-five thousand soldiers whose bodies were never found. Gravesite and deathsite pilgrimages commenced immediately after the war, as soon as it was safe to do so, and that war tourism has continued to this day. It is a kind of homing that is deeply inherent, and non-verbal. Glancing over a map, names mark our knowledge of the torturous suffering of a million men, platoon by platoon at Moorslede, Langemark-Poelkapelle, Poperinghe, Houthulst, Messines, the Thiepval, Zonnebeke, Zillebeke, the Menin Road, the Menin Gate, Polygon Wood, Pilckem Ridge, Ploegsteert Wood, Broonseinde, and Gheluvelt.[10]

Throughout the excursion, our predominant bearing is topographical. It is clear that even minor hillocks would have afforded the troops enormous strategic advantage, which was indeed enjoyed by the German forces on the slightly higher ground. They were able to divert water into the lower British trenches, exacerbating the already horrible conditions. A far view, glimpsed from a warm Volvo, suggests how many thousands of men would fit in a space that could be blanked out with the palm of the outstretched hand; how many could be shred by artillery shells. The gravity of this earthland sounds within the chest, as if a million heartbeats represent a million lives slain. In April the color of the terrain molders between grey and brown; the drizzle is so fine one might call it fog. On a rightly cold, rainy, and windy spring morning,

Kathleen, Rick and I walked through Tyne Cot Cemetery. A headstone reads: "Sacrificed to the fallacy/That war can end war." Twelve thousand graves; eight thousand of which contain men without names: "A Soldier of the Great War—Known Unto God." A video presentation in the Tyne Cot museum names the fallen, during which I had my only moment of emotional choking during my weeks in Flanders, as a picture of a Maori, Te Patariki Faumina, focused the power of malevolence to remove a man from his indigenous location, ship him ten thousand miles into the mud, there to be obscenely slain by the forces of Christian materialist greed and nationalistic bear-baiting.

When we drove into Zillebeke, by some ghostly apposition, I knew what I wanted as soon as we entered the Hill 60 Café: a Jupiler beer, *deux jambons*, a Coca-Cola, coffee with clotted cream, a bowl of *framboises gateau*, hand-cranked vanilla ice cream, and two white martinis. Rick wondered what spirit had made me so audacious in my consumption, and though I could not quite explain it, I knew that it was some matter of grace to experience the warmth of the café and the luxury of the fare, as if on behalf of ghosts.

We then walked around the grounds of Hill 60, which, except for the trees, has been unchanged for nearly a century. I knelt on the dirt path—amid the monuments and pillboxes and crater holes—and picked up a shrapnel ball, one of thousands or millions that had shrieked there, and which had now unburied itself after nine decades. The lead-heavy ball in my hand was the luminous detail of which Professor Hugh Kenner has spoken, and it was the single entirely unmediated event that I could experience in Flanders, where every historian and writer has left his or her impression upon our contemplation. A few days later I lay awake, 3:00 AM in my Roubaix hotel room, and realized that had I lain there in 1917, the deep rumbling of the ceaseless bombardments from eight kilometres away, would have filled my ears and inflected my pulse ever after with the repulsive sounds of slaughter and grief. And had I been in Roubaix trying to sleep, on 27 August 1917, hearing that thunder of evil and despair, I might have become aware that at some moment during that afternoon, across the Atlantic Ocean, in Ithaca, New York, my father was being born. A few hundred yards from his birthplace that very day, the war was set aside by Warner Oland and Lionel Barrymore, who were making movies at the Wharton Studios by the lake of the Cayuga Iroquois, *Tiohero*. Up in an East Hill classroom, Howard Hawks might have pondered the war, as he steeped himself in novels. In five years Vera Brittain would tramp the gorges and waterfalls I would much later myself wander.

By 1917, conceptions of the war in Europe had lost every bit of their always-false notions of glory, the snows fell and a chilling number of new European orphans would define the coming decades with their curious sense of stepfathers, many of whom were themselves bruised veterans. For many soldiers, confections of a benign deity were extinguished in the trenches, yet other chimerae persisted for those of us who prefer to detect personally relevant meridians leading to and out of that war: Dizzy Gillespie, John Lee Hooker, Buddy Rich, and Thelonious Monk were born during the weeks of Passchendaele. Maya Deren, Anthony Burgess, Carson McCullers, and Lena Horne were infants. The Belgian/French Manouche Romani family of Django Reinhardt relocated to suburban Paris during the war, where the jazz guitarist learned the banjo, guitar, and violin in that obscure milieu of gypsy indifference and non-involvement. The Dutch spy Margaretha Geertruida M'greet Zelle MacLeod (Mata Hari) was executed in October during the battle; she was the *femme fatale* to perfection. My father had departed Europe after the Second World War from Brest (after purloining a German motorcycle in Paris and cruising the boulevards, and then, unreally, chatting with Marlene Dietrich in a store, as she shopped for stockings). On the way to Brest, he might have passed through Loudeac, a town founded in 1148, and through which Provençal and Catalunyan troubadours were known to pass on their way to London. Proust knew the town. Just a couple kilometres away from Loudeac, Kerouac's people had departed for Canada. For a few moments in Loudeac, in 1987, taking a nap on the lush lawns of the city park, I slipped into a reverie the likes of which I had not, and have not since, experienced. The nature of the dream was that I was home. Paraphrasing a poem by David Ray, 'I ran up to the place like a lost comrade on a battlefield.' In Flanders, as in Loudeac, as I returned to Ithaca, I experienced deeply the "shock of recognition."

I thought of persons of my acquaintance who had spoken to voices from the war: My uncle Gene McCray served on a naval ship during the First World War. His primary recollection of his service was limited to memory of the girls with whom he'd sported in far ports. As an infant, my friend Cynthia was held in the arms—a blessing—of her grandfather, Charles Waterman Lawry, a month before his death. He had been a battlefield runner who suffered gas poisoning. A friend on Martha's Vineyard, Carol Johanssen, recalls that her grandfather had emigrated from Sweden to America and almost directly into the US Army; he served in France. The grandfather of my British-born physician served with the Household Battalion—The Life Guards in 1916 and 1917; he had been gassed. I had interviewed World War Two Navy veteran John Harrington, whose father was a member of the 1918 Lost Battalion. His father had been wounded, and was one of the very few men to be successfully evacuated. Archival records attest to his ordeal, but he never said a word about it to his son John. My ninety year old Ithaca friend Leon Poelvoorde's mother was in Bruxelles during the war, pressed into service to support the occupying German officers in residence. She was grateful to be allowed to take away the kitchen's potato peels, with which she was able to feed her family.

Other forms and forces may masquerade, but Passchendaele does not exist in the past or in the past tense. By the bombs and murderous conditions, men were disconnected from order; their minds became unbonded. A concussion creates dissociated remembrances, a mother's eye color, and molasses cookies; Bretons perished at Passchendaele, a Ker'ouache first cousin will have boarded a train in Fougeres, bound for Ypres (Kerouac family motto: *Aimer, Travailler, Souffrir*). This convention was for death, and nothing else.

My grandfather in Ithaca read the newspaper on August the 27th, 1917, perhaps contemplated having had an eighth son, and may have spoken aloud or silently, a word he had never heard before: "Passchendaele."

One searches, ever in vain, for a rare triad of sensation that might be called "real in the present tense," the cessation of self-deception, and the unequivocal. A well-remarked phenomenon of the Vietnam War is that soldiers there wanted to be home, and when they returned home, the only thing that seemed real to them was Vietnam. A parallel estrangement has not been mentioned for the First World War, though Sassoon remarked that "the Front was the only place where one could get away from the war." For the most part, its soldiers returned home, and simply burrowed back into their families and their stations of employment. Men survive, especially after trauma, by converting their urge to forget into denial, for to contemplate the millions killed, and the damage it had done to the culture, would have resulted in the tragic, and final, annealing of souls.

Trouble with time. Accounts of the battles by its participants uniformly note the overwhelming symphony of effects and impressions that were aggregated by aspects of the conflict. When not numb with boredom (waiting, marching, waiting) the crescendo of battle was—if not describable—surely for the soldiers an experience they could not instantly process. Their principal focus was on eluding death or damage, and, only to the degree they were capable, following the orders of their officers. Yet most narrative accounts try to suggest the breakdown of sense-discretion that was occasioned by the mind-numbing fear, penetrating cold and wonder, bitter evaporation of the self, horrific onslaughts of sensation, utterly blinding amalgam of physical and mental incapacities, and barely recognizable relics of duration, presence, and self. In several of his books and letters, Robert Briffault has described the conditions and scenes of the war, and he has described what ordeal, privation, and sleep deprivation will do to the cultured unconscious, with especial emphasis on what might otherwise have filled it: the "spirit of twelfth century romanze," and such liberations allowed by a belief in the primacy of matriarchy and unquestioned self-reliance. He marked the war as a pivot in the span of cultural collapse, but our own conception of the war exists outside of time; it is subliminal and immanent. Others might call this Jungian. Proust allows us to form, as we read *In Search of Lost Time*, an almost romantic relationship with such tenses as the *futur-anterieur*, which we may wish to convert into a kind of "time indefinite." Briffault noted that time at the front was "curious; one would be hard put to say whether time passes quickly or slowly—it seems to be slow owing to the weariness & dreariness and yet one is astonished to note how quickly time has passed." The grounds of battle were sealed beneath a dome of suspension and otherness; light and sound came from unexpected directions and dimensions, and a blurred, woolly feeling—as with fever—penetrated men's physical senses and the notion of their own being. The pope of time philosophy, Henri Bergson, spent many of the war months in America, noticing that the war was chiefly, for him, mediated by newspapers, which also existed altogether removed from the present tense. (Perhaps he foresaw media and messages.) Soldiers were compelled to recast their own idiomatic concepts of "duration" and "simultaneity." All readers of Proust notice that the war comes and goes in a flicker, while a mere *aperçu* relating to a bit of fashion occupies several pages of fine discrimination. Wyndham Lewis' 1927 book *Time and Western Man* also questions our fond adherence to the idea that duration and chronology are what we say they are, but by actually *opposing* Bergson's "process philosophy," and its fluidity and synthetic nature. Lewis' war is all about the planes and the surfaces of things; there is nothing you cannot *now* see.

After some years of imprecision, errors of enthusiasm, and discursive reading, the waves of unlocking the clues and leads were furthered when Jean Vogdes Callahan made possible the first understanding in which I had confidence, of books I'd read thirty years earlier: Pound's *Cantos*, Briffault, and she shined true light on every page of Proust, so that I could regard the ultimate measure of aesthetic truth to be the beautiful rhythm of the perfectly confected prose sentence. This prose, wherever I found it, might have a bewildering number of subordinate clauses and parenthetical asides, but the language was always pure and relevant. Vogdes had looked more deeply into "close reading" than I had ever imagined it was possible to do, and therefore unlocked the tangle of undifferentiated information I had gathered about persons in extreme conditions; as in the war.

I am interested in the social aspects of the war, and the effects of the war on collective human nature. I was born just thirty years after Passchendaele, and my first glimmers of apperception came through and are forever indebted to Marshal McLuhan, who directed his attention to the most important fact of the twentieth century: the methodology of apperception, the morning truth of the modern novel. I therefore regard the battle at Third Ypres through the media and literary context. Anyone comes to the war by a personal route of empathy. This battle and this war and these impossible scenes are for us displays of our imagination, as that has been nourished and shaped by ninety thousand hours of watching a housefront fall on Buster Keaton, and its endless versions and equivalents. In graduate school at Chapel Hill I studied Medieval Romance and the Arthurian grail legends; should I see these soldiers as Parzivals? Henry James died during the Battle of Verdun. Gaudier-Brzeska was killed during an act of conspicuous bravery. Briffault eluded death at Passchendaele. Put into words truly.

Though I suppose I had vaguely understood that it was somewhat similar to the process of empathy, I had not known that the biographical enterprise could be very personally thrilling until the peerless American biographer Stacy Schiff handed me a copy of Richard Holmes' *Footsteps*, the first chapter of which on Robert Louis Stevenson well explains the sort of exhilaration of the gold-mining research and scholarship Stacy had herself experienced while tracking a single line of her sympathetic eloquence from Antoine Saint-Exupery through Vera Nabokov, Benjamin Franklin, Cleopatra, and the Salem witches. As a somewhat similar identifying trek appeared before me, Robert Briffault's expansive and complex chart of biography, bibliography, and assessment became to me, personal. Not necessarily a man to be admired, Briffault did coalesce as no one had before, the chief lighthouses by which I had been assuming I might be able to navigate my course.

I now reread Ford's tetralogy in a sort of nostalgia for the moments of my originally discovering the lighting that I took to be true. In this I count myself among companions who have accomplished their resolution of ambivalences by establishing magnetic north in the episode by which monstrously large forces were enwrapped by monstrous stupidity: The Great War. The war was a function of the course of man, with its fulfillment of man's innate desire to kill perceived predators, an appetite never slaked. For me, understanding the war was both recognition and a dismantling of cliché. It is now impossible to imagine my life without ever having empathized my way into a putrid ratty trench of no equivocation.

This verse play nominates one twenty-first century caste of individuals who have completely removed themselves from the possibility of understanding why they might either choose to join or be sucked into a remote war. They have excused themselves from the possibility of being betrayed, or supporting some vain nationalist or geopolitical cause. They have removed themselves from even the dimmest recollection of what 1914-1918 might have been about. I think of them as dharma bums, and an arc flows from the German boys and the British boys, and all their allied savaged kinfolk, to those who are separated, disaffected, detached, and aloof, and who refuse to accept an inherited state of affairs. This tribe of outcasts, romanisch, vagabonds, streetkids, hoboes, bums, indifferent marginals, the blissfully undefined, and passive anarchists—perhaps like the artists whose work was birthed around the First World War and who did not feel (necessarily) beholden to the artists who had come before—nurtures a world culture that makes nation-states as obsolete as some consortium of not-for-profits and NGOs like UNICEF or medecins sans frontiers—and this tribe is best understood by another tribe, one composed of soldiers buried in a muddy trench for no reason they will ever understand. The moral result of the mad war is alive within us, and it has enabled some persons to come in a quite different manner to be audaciously separate.

It seems to me almost impossible to believe that in the first few days after I started college in a green and leafy upstate New York village in

1965, I would meet three other students who would leave upon me the sort of effect and difference that goes, honorably, by the name profound. This effect is not uncommon, going off to college, but neither is it ever dismissible.

The lyrics were written specifically for Andrew Doyle's voice—his manner and inflection and humor—the fellow I met that day twenty years after the end of the Second World War, and the same I was to meet forty-five years after that, in Ithaca. My initial cultural tutorials were with Andrew, as I watched him weave the plots of plays, and as he signaled the end of the moribund post World War II years with his often-outrageous theatrical acts. Another shock of recognition occurred when I looked across the quadrangle and saw a girl wearing flowered stockings. A day or so before that I had read a note she had left for the person who had stolen her umbrella that rainy day, a note of the very finest satire, which I had before not known existed outside of books. She instantly contextualized everything, to her infinite pain, but she added a crucial facet to my view of the world. And an outré fellow named Terry Gore arrived at college that day virtually besotted with his obsession with medieval warfare, and even then, in the mid 1960s just out of high school, had studied and knew more of his subject than many scholars.[11]

What a strange wonder they had been able to then suggest. Andrew was theatrically gifted, and charismatic. Terry had long hair, wore leather boots, brought a television to the dormitory, drank often, smoked marijuana, could read Hebrew, crafted a fifteen foot, lead-figured, topographically correct board game replica of Agincourt, bore randy tattoos (all of this at eighteen years old, 1965) and was fabulously besotted by rambunctious monkey-sex with his girlfriend Sloopy. The girl across the quadrangle was beautiful and sultrily suggestive; I would come to know her well, and learn that her mind was lost in invisible structures. I had not realized until many years later, that she had been severed from time, and was, to her immense pain, unable to prevent the simultaneity of her present and her future. But she had known—probably since she was a little girl—that she need not adhere to her own present. "Be here now," and "this too shall pass," had no meaning for her, and were, in fact, rhetorical insults to her temporal fluency.

All three of my new friends possessed matchless and mystical intellectual maturities that I had not previously seen in the flesh. A half-century passed, and now I find myself imagining that Andrew's accomplishments, lived wholly through the spectrum of the arts, and Candace's fearsomely sagacious and over-abundantly contextualizing mind, and Terry's locating the signal and most elemental nature of man in warfare, are the spirits guiding my reading, and therefore myself. With them I aggregated the means to see the truth of the Great War—through bicycling's independence and poetry's indifference to objectivity—that the tragic flaw of mankind was venality and suborning: enticing others to commit crimes, against their better natures.

The 1960s and subsequent years had at the time seemed to me a hurricane blowing away the effete patterns and elements of the past— bombing and blasting away the pretensions and vain rhetorics of almost everything that had been founded before the end of the Second World War. I was, then, pickled in the bright, loud rainstorm of contemporaneity. But I experienced the late twentieth century's central trick, and slowly and then all at once recognized that the bibliography of artists and dancers and painters and writers to whom I paid the most attention, upon whose earth I had planted my flag, had made their works having directly participated in some version of Passchendaele: a vain, bloody expression of evil. As against which, my lighthearted and ahistoric self-determination seemed a vacant frivolity.

I permit myself the rhetorical reverie that all along the years these three had been trying to point me to Third Ypres, Passchendaele, where there had been a core moment, and at least one hard answer: here ye fight, or here ye die, thine own self. Assaying mid the wreckage, my wonderment searches for just the thing that in the 1960s we thought we were demanding: relevance. This presence of peace rhymed with just the moment I heard the lyric: *at Passchendaele the mud was oceanic . . .*

Ypres, 1917.

First day of the battle of the Somme, July 1, 1916.

Victims of gas, 1918.

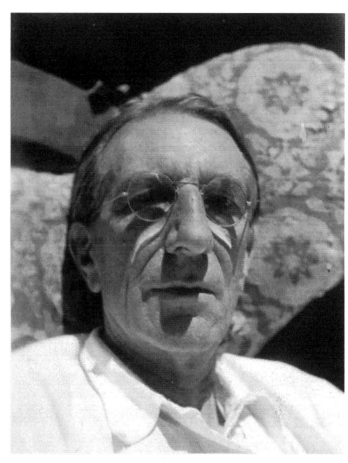

Robert Briffault, 1873–1948.

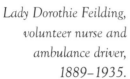

*Lady Dorothie Feilding,
volunteer nurse and
ambulance driver,
1889–1935.*

*Mary Borden, founder of
the Hadfield-Spears
Ambulance Unit,
1886–1968.*

Siegfried Sassoon, British pacifist, soldier, and author, 1886–1967.

Charles Waterman Lawry, American runner, 1897–1957.

*Henri-Alban Fournier
(the author
Alain-Fournier)
1886–1914.*

Vera Brittain, Voluntary Aid Detachment nurse, and author, 1893–1970.

Henri Gaudier-Brzeska, sculptor, 1891–1915.

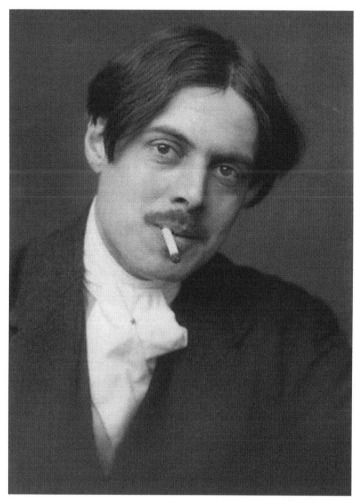

Wyndham Lewis, 1882–1957.

The Vorticist literary magazine BLAST
(editor Wyndham Lewis), 1915.

A Battery Shelled, *Wyndham Lewis, 1919.*

Stormtroopers Advancing Under Cover of Gas, *Otto Dix, 1924.*

Wounded Soldier, *Otto Dix, 1916.*

Author Notes

[1] Herma Briffault was an important translator into English of Colette, Albert Camus, and Ho Chi Minh, thereby providing an important flavor of the language by which these three original thinkers were perceived by mid-twentieth century readers.

[2] In the First World War, Lister Briffault, at age eighteen, was a pilot of a Maurice Farman biplane for the Royal Naval Air Service; he then flew with the Royal Air Force, and was awarded the Military Medal for Bravery. He survived the war and returned to New Zealand.

[3] Portugal was well-involved with the Entente forces during the war, but Spain remained importantly neutral. Bruised by the recent Spanish-American War, Spain and its colonies provided material support to both sides.

[4] Vera Brittain was a pacifist and feminist, and in a charm of vindication and justice, her humane work prevails to this day in the form of her daughter, Shirley Williams, a Labour MP and member of the "Gang of Four" who co-founded the Social Democrat Party, which eventually formed a coalition with the Liberal Party to become the Liberal Democrats. Williams was also a professor at Harvard and a BBC television political host.

[5] https://archive.org/details/aphysicianinfra00herrgoog

[6] http://www.westernfrontassociation.com/
http://www.ww1ha.org/

[7]   See also *The Last Veteran, Harry Patch and the Legacy of War*, by Peter Parker and *Last of the Doughboys* by Richard Rubin.

[8]   An important collection of Vera Brittain's papers is also at McMaster. Archive http://library.mcmaster.ca/archives/findaids/findaids/b/briffaul.htm

[9]   Washington's orders: "The Expedition you are appointed to command is to be directed against the hostile tribes of the Six Nations of Indians, with their associates and adherents. The immediate objects are the total destruction and devastation of their settlements, and the capture of as many prisoners of every age and sex as possible. It will be essential to ruin their crops now in the ground and prevent their planting more. I would recommend, that some post in the center of the Indian Country, should be occupied with all expedition, with a sufficient quantity of provisions whence parties should be detached to lay waste all the settlements around, with instructions to do it in the most effectual manner, that the country may not be merely overrun, but destroyed. But you will not by any means listen to any overture of peace before the total ruinment of their settlements is effected [sic]. Our future security will be in their inability to injure us and in the terror with which the severity of the chastisement they receive will inspire them."

[10]   *Gheluvelt* is a word of especial ugliness, that inspires the father of a killed soldier to venture from Vancouver Island to Belgium to see the spot where his son was lost. Viz. W. D. Wetherell's book *A Century of November*.

[11]   Terry L. Gore, *Neglected Heroes: Leadership and War in the Early Medieval Period* (Westport, CT: Praeger Publishers, 1995).

References

Full sources are given in the notes only when the source is not obvious from the text or bibliography. Multi-part quotes may extend onto the next page.

p. 3   "As a man of imagination . . ." Arthur Searle, "Preface," (London: Letters of Robert Briffault Collection, British Library 1977).

p. 4   "abominated Mozart and Bach. . . ." Lawrence F. Koons notes, in the Robert Briffault Collection, William Ready Division of Archives and Research Collections, McMaster University Library (Hamilton, ON: typescript, unpaginated).

p. 5   "Like everyone else, Estorick . . ." Lawrence F. Koons, "Preface," *The Troubadours* by Robert Briffault.

p. 6   "Malrika had spent the war years . . ." Koons notes, Robert Briffault Collection.

p. 6   "I kiss you in a place . . ." ibid.

p. 8   "Puritan tradition, combined . . ." Robert Briffault, *Sin and Sex* (London: George Allen and Unwin, Ltd. 1931), p. 119.

p. 9   "It is the highest honour . . ." Searle, "Preface," British Library.

p. 10   "It was under the influence . . ." Robert Briffault, *The Making of Humanity* (London: George Allen & Unwin, 1919).

p. 14   "the War has stopped Art dead . . ." W. K. Rose, *The Letters of Wyndham Lewis*, p. 69. (Letter to Kate Lechmere.)

p. 16   "These apparently rude and brutal . . ." Frederic Manning, *The Middle Parts of Fortune, Somme and Ancre*, p. 205.

p. 17   "perhaps the war had made . . ." The Official Site of the Stuart Cloete Literary Estate, "The War Years 1914–1918," sponsored by Stuart Cloete Literary Holdings, Ltd.   http://www.stuartcloete.com/biography/31/the-war-years-1914–1918 (accessed June 24, 2014).

p. 19   "The only treatment . . ." Walker Percy, *Love in the Ruins* (NY: Farrar Strauss Giroux, Noonday, 1971), p. 37.

p. 19   "One had a vague feeling . . ." Manning, p. 209.

p. 20   "It was life rather than death . . ." Llewelyn Wyn Griffith, *Up to Mametz and Beyond*, p. 109.

p. 23   "nothing gets exhausted so quickly . . ." Lewis Dabney, *Edmund Wilson: A Life in Literature* (NY: Farrar, Strauss and Giroux, 2005), p. 58.

p. 26   "The conditions in which we filmed. . ." Kevin Brownlow, *The Parade's Gone By . . .* (London: Columbus Books, 1989; first publ. 1968), p. 533.

p. 26   "entering its thirty-fourth month . . ." F. H. Simonds, *History of the World War*, p. vi.

p. 27   "Dear, dear Mitsou . . ." Colette, *Mitsou*, p. 62.

p. 28   "democracy of the dead . . ." Noble Foster Hoggson, *Just Behind the Front*, p. 121.

p. 28   "a holocaust . . ." Ibid., 121.

p. 31   "During this period my indebtedness . . ." Edmund Blunden, *Undertones of War*, p. 170.

p. 32   "the situation is obscure. . . ." J. C. Dunn, *The War the Infantry Knew: 1914–1919*, p. 466.

p. 32   "no one who matters . . ." Ibid., 434.

p. 32   "Next we learned . . ." Ibid., p. 298.

p. 32   "some dilettante . . ." Ibid., p. 276.

p. 32   "A bad blister . . ." Ibid., p. 314.

p. 32   "made a noise like wind . . ." Ibid., p. 229.

p. 33   "doubts if the men here are. . ." Ibid., p. 453.

p. 34   "Courage remained . . ." Siegfried Sassoon, *The Complete Memoirs of George Sherston*, p. 230.

p. 34   "that big, bullying bogey. . . ." Ibid., p. 266.

p. 34   "had watched an army of ghosts. . . ." Ibid., p. 362.

p. 35   "I walked about the room . . ." Ibid., p. 377.

p. 35   "I am making this statement . . ." Ibid., p. 496.

p. 36   "humanity had been outraged . . ." Ibid., p. 557.

p. 37   "Art has no inside . . ." Wyndham Lewis, *Tarr* (London: *The Egoist*, 1918), p. 295.

p. 37   "the preparations for Passchendaele . . ." Wyndham Lewis, *Blasting and Bombardiering*, p. 151.

p. 38   "I must join the Army. . . ." Rose, p. 73.

p. 38   "I think I told you . . ." Ibid., p. 92.

p. 39   "On the battlefield of France . . ." Wyndham Lewis, *Rude Assignment* (London: Hutchinson and Company, 1950), p. 149.

p. 39   "which sterilized . . ." Vera Brittain, *Testament of Youth*, p. 37.

p. 40   "There is something so starved . . ." Ibid., p. 211.

p. 40   "I went up Denmark Hill . . ." Ibid., p. 262.

p. 40   "Between 1914 and 1918 . . ." Ibid., p. 370.

p. 41   "No doubt the post-war generation . . ." Ibid., p. 490.

p. 43   "From Hugo's novel . . ." Edmund Wilson, *I Thought of Daisy*, p. 48.

p. 44   "Since the War . . ." Ibid., p. 55.

p. 45   "There was a man . . ." Mary Borden, "Blind," in *The Forbidden Zone*, p. 94.

p. 47   "[Woolf] saw its experience . . ." Karen L. Levenback, *Virginia Woolf and the Great War*, p. 1.

p. 48   "In Zonnebeke . . ." John Ellis, *Eye-Deep in Hell*, p. 24.

p. 48   "One evening whilst on patrol . . ." Ibid., p. 55.

p. 48   "A variety of sounds . . ." Ibid., p. 65.

p. 50   "The months pass by. . . ." Erich Maria Remarque, *All Quiet on the Western Front*, p. 236.

p. 51   "That which was achieved . . ." Jack Sheldon, *The German Army at Passchendaele*, p. 29.

p. 52   "Heavy shellfire . . ." Ibid., p. 149.

p. 52   "Only the newspapers in England . . ." Ibid., p. 251.

p. 52   "A lot of what has been . . ." Ibid., p. 252.

p. 53   " sunset all seraphim and cherubim. . . ." Winston Groom, *A Storm in Flanders*, p. 205.

p. 54   "Strength was equated . . ." George L. Mosse, *Fallen Soldiers*, p. 58.

p. 58   "I noticed how loudly . . ." Philip Gibbs, *Now it Can Be Told*, p. 15.

p. 58   "the most beautiful book ever written . . ." *Le Libertaire* (presumed 1930). Quotation from *Le Libertaire* found on the back cover of *Fear* by Gabriel Chevallier published in 2011. The quote is considered to be from a review of the original book in French by Gabriel Chevallier, *La Peur*, self-published in 1920.

p. 59   "Men are foolish and ignorant. . . ." Gabriel Chevallier, *Fear* (London: Profile Books, 2012), p 7. Translated by Malcolm Imrie.

p. 63   "In a strange street by night . . ." Norbert Wolf and Uta Grosenick, *Expressionism*, (Cologne: Taschen, 2004), p. 42.

p. 64   "at the front . . ." Fritz Kreisler, *Four Weeks in the Trenches*, p. 6.

p. 64   "the crudeness, variety . . ." Gilles Neret, *Fernand Leger* (London: Alpine Fine Arts, 1993), p. 66. (Quoted from Fernand Leger diary.)

p. 68   "it would be dangerous for . . ." David Burnett-James, *Ravel* (London: Omnibus Press, 1983), p. 83.

p. 70   "Our woods are magnificent . . ." Ezra Pound, *Gaudier-Brzeska*, p. 69.

p. 75   "I adore war. . . ." John Nauright and Timothy J.L. Chandler, eds., *Making Men: Rugby and Masculine Identify* (London: Frank Cass & Co. LTD, 1996), p. 151. (From a letter to his parents in October 1914.)

p. 76   "I suppose you think the war . . ." Samuel Hynes, *A War Imagined* (New York: Atheneum, 1991) p. 266. (D. H. Lawrence quoted by Samuel Hynes.)

p. 79   "The War bled the world white. . . ." Wyndham Lewis, *Blasting and Bombardiering*, p. 17.

p. 79   "However this is enough . . ." Ibid., p. 342.

p. 83   "When the war ended, I don't know if I was more relieved . . ." Harry Patch interview in *The Sunday Times*, 7 November 2004.

p. 83   "I was with him for the last . . ." Ibid.

p. 83   "The beasts had a curious effect . . ." Paul O'Keeffe, *Gaudier-Brzeska*, p. 152.

p. 86   "The country around Ypres . . ." Letters of Robert Briffault, (London: British Library, manuscript, unpaginated).

p. 92   "Julian walked back . . ." Robert Briffault, *Europa in Limbo*, p. 290–294.

p. 167   "I had never before been . . ." Alain-Fournier, *The Lost Estate*, p. 148.

p. 168   "demented language . . ." Sassoon, *George Sherston*, p. 450.

p. 176   "the Front was the only place . . ." Ibid., p. 456.

p. 177   "curious; one would be . . ." Letters of Robert Briffault, British Library.

SELECT BIBLIOGRAPHY

Alain-Fournier. *The Lost Estate (Le Grand Meaulnes)*. London: Penguin Books Ltd., 2007.

Babington, Anthony. *Shell-Shock: A History of the Changing Attitudes to War Neurosis*. Barnsley, UK: Pen and Sword Books, 1997.

Barbusse, Henri. *Under Fire: The Story of a Squad (Le Feu)*. New York: Dutton, 1916.

Barker, Pat. *Regeneration*. London: Penguin Books, 1991.

Beck, James M. *The Evidence in the Case as to the Moral Responsibility for the War*. New York: Grosset & Dunlap Publishers, 1915.

Bird, Will R. *Ghosts Have Warm Hands: A Memoir of the Great War, 1916-1919*. Toronto: Clarke, Irwin, 1968.

Borden, Mary. *The Forbidden Zone*. London: Hesperus Press Limited, 2008.

——. *Flamingo*. Garden City: Doubleday, Page & Company, 1927.

Blunden, Edmund. *Undertones of War*. Chicago: University of Chicago Press, 2007.

Briffault, Robert. *Fandango*. New York: Charles Scribner's Sons, 1940.

——. *Europa*. New York: Charles Scribner's Sons, 1935.

——. *Europa in Limbo*. New York: Charles Scribner's Sons, 1937.

——. *The Mothers–The Matriarchal Theory of Social Origins*. New York: Grosset & Dunlap, The Universal Library, 1963.

——. *The New Life of Mr. Martin*. New York: Charles Scribner's Sons, 1947.

——. *The Troubadours*. Bloomington: Indiana University Press, 1965.

Brittain, Vera. *Testament of Youth*. London: Penguin Books, 2005.

——. *Testament of Friendship*. London: Virago Press, 1997.

Chevallier, Gabriel. *Fear*. London: Profile Books, 2012.

Coetzee, Frans, and Shevin-Coetzee, Marilyn. *World War I: A History in Documents*. Oxford: Oxford University Press, 2002.

Colette. *Mitsou*. New York: Avon Publications, Inc., 1957.

Conway, Jane. *A Woman of Two Wars: The Life of Mary Borden*. London: Munday Books, 2010.

Cummings, E. E. *The Enormous Room*. New York: Liveright, 1978.

Dunn, J. C. *The War the Infantry Knew: 1914–1919*. London, UK: Abacus, Time Warner Book Group UK, 1994.

Dyer, Geoff. *The Missing of the Somme*. London: Penguin Books, 1994.

Ede, H. S. *Savage Messiah: A Biography of the Scultor Henri Gaudier-Brezska*. Leeds: Henry Moore Institute Publications, 2011.

Eksteins, Modris. *Rites of Spring: The Great War and the Birth of the Modern Age*. Boston: Houghton Mifflin Company, 2000.

Ellis, John. *Eye-Deep in Hell: Trench Warfare in World War I*. Baltimore: Johns Hopkins University Press, 1977.

Elton, Ben. *The First Casualty*. London: Bantam Press, 2005.

Empey, Arthur Guy. *Over the Top*. New York: G. P. Putnam's Sons, The Knickerbocker Press, 1917.

Englund, Peter. *The Beauty and the Sorrow: An Intimate History of the First World War*. London: Profile Books Ltd., 2011.

Ferguson, Niall. *The Pity of War*. London: Perseus Books, 1999.

Ford, Ford Madox. *The Good Soldier*. New York: Vintage Books, Random House, 1957.

——. *Parade's End*. London: Penguin Books, 2001.

Fussell, Paul. *The Great War and Modern Memory*. Oxford: Oxford University Press, 2000.

——. *Abroad*. Oxford: Oxford University Press, 1980.

Gibbs, Philip. *Now It Can Be Told*. New York: Harper and Brothers, 1920.

Gilbert, Adrian. *World War I in Photographs*. London: Military Press, 1986.

Graves, Robert. *Good-bye to All That*. Garden City: Doubleday Anchor Books, 1957.

Griffith, Llewelyn Wyn. *Up to Mametz and Beyond*. Barnsley, UK: Pen and Sword Books, 2010.

Groom, Winston. *A Storm in Flanders*. New York: Atlantic Monthly Press, 2002.

Gross, Paul. *Passchendaele*. Toronto: HarperCollins Publishers Ltd., 2008.

Hart, Liddell. *The War in Outline: 1914–1918*. New York: Random House, 1936.

Hašek, Jaroslav. *The Good Soldier Švejk*. London: Penguin Books, 2000.

Hochschild, Adam. *To End All Wars: a Story of Loyalty and Rebellion, 1914–1918*. New York: Houghton Mifflin Harcourt Publishing Company, 2011.

Hoggson, Noble Foster. *Just Behind the Front*. New York: John Lane Company, 1918.

Holmes, Richard. *Tommy: The British Soldier on the Western Front, 1914–1918*. London: Harper Perennial, 2005.

Joll, James. *The Origins of the First World War*. London: Longman, 1989.

Jünger, Ernst. *Storm of Steel*. London: Penguin Books, 2003.

Kreisler, Fritz. *Four Weeks in the Trenches: The War Story of a Violinist*. New York: Houghton, Mifflin Company, 1915.

Levenback, Karen L. *Virginia Woolf and the Great War*. Syracuse: Syracuse University Press, 1999.

Lewis, Wyndham. *Blasting and Bombardiering*. Berkeley: University of California Press, 1967.

Macdonald, Lyn. *To the Last Man: Spring 1918*. New York: Carroll & Graf Publishers, Inc., 1998.

——. *The Roses of No Man's Land*. London: Penguin Books, 1993.

——. *They Called it Passchendaele*. London: Penguin Books, 1978.

——. *Somme*. London: Penguin Books, 1983.

——. *1915: The Death of Innocence*. Baltimore: Johns Hopkins University Press, 2000.

——. *1914–1918: Voices and Images of the Great War*. London: Penguin Books, 1991.

Macintyre, Ben. *The Englishman's Daughter*. New York: Delta Publishing, Random House, 2002.

Mackin, Elton E. *Suddenly We Didn't Want to Die: Memoirs of a World War I Marine*. Novato, CA: Presidio Press, 1996.

Manning, Frederic. *The Middle Parts of Fortune, Somme and Ancre, 1916*. New York: Penguin Books, 1990.

Matloff, Maurice, editor. *World War I: A Concise Military History of "The War to End All Wars" and the Road to the War*. New York: David McKay Company, Inc., 1979.

Meyers, Jeffrey. *The Enemy: A Biography of Wyndham Lewis*. Boston: Routledge & Kegan Paul, 1982.

Michel, Walter. *Wyndham Lewis: Paintings and Drawings*. Berkeley: University of California Press, 1969.

Michel, Walter, editor. *Wyndham Lewis on Art*. New York: Funk & Wagnalls, 1969.

Montague, C.E. *Disenchantment*. London: Chatto & Windus, 1922.

Moorhouse, Geoffrey. *Hell's Foundations*. New York: Henry Holt and Company, 1992.

Mosse, George L. *Fallen Soldiers: Reshaping the Memory of the World Wars*. Oxford: Oxford University Press, 1990.

Nicolson, Juliet. *The Perfect Summer*. New York: Grove Press, 2006.

——. *The Great Silence*. New York: Grove Press, 2009.

O'Keeffe, Paul. *Gaudier-Brzeska: An Absolute Case of Genius*. London: Allen Lane, Penguin Books, 2004.

Patch, Harry, and Van Emden, Richard. *The Last Fighting Tommy: The Life of Harry Patch, Last Veteran of the Trenches, 1898–2009*. London: Bloomsbury, 2007.

Parker, Peter. *The Last Veteran: Harry Patch and the Legacy of War*. London: Fourth Estate, HarperCollins Publishers, 2009.

Pound, Ezra. *Gaudier-Brzeska*. New York: New Directions Publishing Company, 1970.

Prior, Robin, and Wilson, Trevor. *Passchendaele: the Untold Story*. New Haven: Yale University Press, 2002.

Remarque, Erich Maria. *All Quiet on the Western Front*. New York: Bantam Books, 1985.

Rose, W. K., editor. *The Letters of Wyndham Lewis*. Norfolk: New Directions Publishing Company, 1963.

Rubin, Richard. *The Last of the Doughboys*. Boston: Houghton Mifflin Harcourt, 2013.

Sassoon, Siegfried. *The Complete Memoirs of George Sherston*. London: Faber and Faber, 1972.

——. *Memoirs of an Infantry Officer*. London: Faber and Faber, 1983.

Sheldon, Jack. *The German Army at Passchendaele*. Barnsley, UK: Pen & Sword Books, Ltd., 2007.

Simonds, F. H. *History of the World War*. New York: Doubleday, 1917.

Strachan, Hew. *World War I: A History*. Oxford: Oxford University Press, 1998.

Suskind, Richard. *Do You Want to Live Forever!* New York: Bantam Books, 1964.

Taylor, A. J. P. *The First World War: An Illustrated History*. New York: Perigee Books, 1980.

Tuchman, Barbara W. *The Guns of August*. New York: Presidio Press, 2004.

Ward, Candace, editor. *World War One British Poets*. Mineola, New York: Dover Publications, 1997.

Warner, Philip. *Passchendaele*. Barnsley, UK: Pen and Sword Classics, 2005.

Wetherell, W. D. *A Century of November*. Ann Arbor: University of Michigan Press, 2007.

Wilson, Edmund. *I Thought of Daisy*. New York: Charles Scribner's Sons, 1929.

——. *The Twenties*. New York: Farrar, Strauss and Giroux, 1979.

Winter, Denis. *Death's Men, Soldiers of the Great War*. London: Penguin Books, 1978.

Wolff, Leon. *In Flanders Fields: the 1917 Campaign*. New York: Viking Press, 1958.

PHIL McCRAY is a graduate of the Iowa Writers'
Workshop, has been a Cornell University manuscripts
archivist, a bicyclist, and founder of the Loudeac
Tile Studio. His next book is a novelized social
history of the nineteenth-century boat bums, scow
tramps, and barge hobos who lived on the Erie Canal.
He was born and lives in Ithaca, New York.

34053164R00126

Made in the USA
Charleston, SC
26 September 2014